THE INCREDIBLE BOOK OF
USELESS
INFORMATION

THE INCREDIBLE BOOK OF
USELESS
INFORMATION

Even More Pointlessly
Unnecessary Knowledge

DON VOORHEES

A PERIGEE BOOK

A PERIGEE BOOK
Published by the Penguin Group
Penguin Group (USA) Inc.
375 Hudson Street, New York, New York 10014, USA

Penguin Group (Canada), 90 Eglinton Avenue East, Suite 700, Toronto, Ontario M4P 2Y3, Canada
(a division of Pearson Penguin Canada Inc.) • Penguin Books Ltd., 80 Strand, London WC2R 0RL,
England • Penguin Group Ireland, 25 St. Stephen's Green, Dublin 2, Ireland (a division of Penguin
Books Ltd.) • Penguin Group (Australia), 250 Camberwell Road, Camberwell, Victoria 3124, Australia
(a division of Pearson Australia Group Pty. Ltd.) • Penguin Books India Pvt. Ltd., 11 Community
Centre, Panchsheel Park, New Delhi—110 017, India • Penguin Group (NZ), 67 Apollo Drive,
Rosedale, Auckland 0632, New Zealand (a division of Pearson New Zealand Ltd.) • Penguin Books
(South Africa) (Pty.) Ltd., 24 Sturdee Avenue, Rosebank, Johannesburg 2196, South Africa

Penguin Books Ltd., Registered Offices: 80 Strand, London WC2R 0RL, England

While the author has made every effort to provide accurate telephone numbers, Internet addresses,
and other contact information at the time of publication, neither the publisher nor the author
assumes any responsibility for errors, or for changes that occur after publication. Further, the
publisher does not have any control over and does not assume any responsibility for author or
third-party websites or their content.

First edition: October 2012

Library of Congress Cataloging-in-Publication Data

Voorhees, Don.
The incredible book of useless information / even more pointlessly
unnecessary knowledge / Don Voorhees.
p.   cm.
"A Perigee book."
ISBN 978-0-399-53746-2
1. Questions and answers.   I. Title.
AG195.V647   2012   2012019795
031.02—dc23

PRINTED IN THE UNITED STATES OF AMERICA

10 9 8 7 6 5 4 3 2 1

Most Perigee books are available at special quantity discounts for bulk purchases for sales
promotions, premiums, fund-raising, or educational use. Special books, or book excerpts, can also
be created to fit specific needs. For details, write: Special Markets, Penguin Group (USA) Inc.,
375 Hudson Street, New York, New York 10014.

*Dedicated to all you lovers
of "useless" information and* Jeopardy! *contestant wannabes.
Enjoy!*

CONTENTS

MASCOT MUSINGS

Squirrels only swim when absolutely necessary. When they do, they do the "doggie paddle," using their tail as a rudder.

Squirrels communicate by making shrill "tchrring" sounds and by moving their tails.

The hair of Canadian red squirrels is used to make cosmetic brushes.

Squirrels defend an area of one to seven acres.

There are sixteen species of chipmunks native to the United States, while there are only eight native squirrel species.

Squirrels control their body temperature with their tails.

Squirrels have yellow-tinted eye lenses that act like sunglasses.

Tree squirrels can turn their back feet completely around when climbing down a tree headfirst.

Marmots are large squirrels.

STAR SEARCH

PRUDISH PERFORMERS

Mila Kunis auditioned "bottom" doubles for her role in the film *Friends with Benefits*. The girls had to line up and bare their behinds to find a good match for use as a double for Kunis in the flick.

Olivia Wilde wore pasties for her sex scene in the film *The Change-Up*. Nipples were digitally added later. Wilde was given the choice of seven different nipple types to pick from.

In the film *Machete*, Jessica Alba wore underwear in the shower scene, which were digitally removed later to make her look nude.

Meryl Streep's body double in *Death Becomes Her* was Catherine Bell, who went on to star in *JAG* and *The Last Man Standing*.

Julia Roberts had a more curvaceous body double stand in for her in *Pretty Woman*.

Kevin Costner had a body double for the nude waterfall scene in *Robin Hood: Prince of Thieves*.

CAN'T GET ENOUGH

Three well-known, self-professed Hollywood sex addicts are Russell Brand, David Duchovny, and Rob Lowe.

Brand once employed a "team of experts" to recruit random women for him to have sex with, before he entered rehab for his problem.

Duchovny, who went through sex addiction rehab in 2008, now stars, ironically, in the Showtime TV program *Californication*, which features plentiful sex and nudity.

Lowe confessed to not being able to go longer than thirty hours without sex.

THE SKINNY

Among the famous people who have publicly admitted to having battled bulimia are Elton John, Jane Fonda, Paula Abdul, Jessica Alba, Calista Flockhart, and Princess Diana.

THE HEARTBREAK

Some well-known sufferers of psoriasis include Jerry Mathers (The Beaver), Stacy London of *What Not to Wear*, LeAnn Rimes, and Kim Kardashian, who has the skin disease on her legs.

HEAVY BREATHERS

Among the stars who have suffered from asthma are Lindsay Lohan, Jason Alexander, Billy Joel, Christopher Reeve, Elizabeth Taylor, Sharon Stone, Diane Keaton, Martin Scorsese, Liza Minnelli, and rapper DMX.

STAR POWER

Tom Brady and Gisele Bündchen were the richest celebrity couple from May 2010 to May 2011, according to *Forbes* magazine. Their combined $75 million income knocked reigning champs Jay-Z and Beyoncé from the top spot.

Lady Gaga ranked number eleven on the *Forbes* list of most powerful women in 2011. At twenty-five, she was the youngest female to crack the list. She was three spots below Michelle Obama and three above Oprah Winfrey.

Forbes magazine listed Leonardo DiCaprio as the highest-paid actor between May 2010 and May 2011, having earned $77 million. Johnny Depp came in second at $50 million.

Sarah Jessica Parker and Angelina Jolie were named the highest-earning actresses by *Forbes* for the period May 2010 through May 2011, each earning about $30 million before attorney and agent fees were deducted.

The highest-paid man in the entertainment business from May 2010 through May 2011 was actor-producer-director Tyler Perry at $130 million, followed by producer Jerry Bruckheimer at $113 million.

Charlie Sheen was the highest-paid performer on television in 2010, making almost $2 million per episode of *Two and a Half Men*. His comedic partner on the show, Jon Cryer, managed to get by on $550,000 per episode.

Marcia Cross, Teri Hatcher, Felicity Huffman, and Eva Longoria each earned $400,000 per episode for starring in *Desperate Housewives*.

Dan Castellaneta and Julie Kavner of *The Simpsons*, likewise, receive $400,000 per show.

Hugh Laurie of *House* earned $400,000-plus per episode.

David Letterman is the late night talk show top dog, pulling down $28 million a year, followed by Jay Leno at $25 million and Conan O'Brien at $10 million.

Matt Lauer of *Today* tops the morning talkers with a salary of more than $16 million per year.

In 2010, evening news personality salaries were led by Katie Couric's $15 million per year, followed by Brian Williams at $12.5 million, Diane Sawyer at $12 million, and Fox News commentator Bill O'Reilly at $10 million.

On the reality show front, Kate Gosselin of *Kate Plus 8* somehow got by on $250,000 a show, and Snooki of *Jersey Shore* raked in $30,000 per episode.

KILLER CLEAVAGE

In 2011, Israeli model Orit Fox was bitten on her left surgically enhanced breast by a snake while attempting to lick said reptile during a radio show stunt. Fox was fine, but the poor snake died soon afterward, from acute silicone poisoning.

BUYER'S REMORSE

Among the celebrities who have publicly stated they regret getting boob jobs are Denise Richards, Tori Spelling, Tara Reid, Sharon Osbourne, Heidi Montag, Jenna Jameson, Victoria Beckham, and Kourtney Kardashian.

INITIALLY YOURS

Johnny Carson's first three wives were named Jody, Joanne, and Joanna. He joked that he married three women with similar first names so that he could keep the same monogrammed towels.

HOLLYWOOD CONFIDENTIAL

Leonardo DiCaprio was fired from the onetime kids' show *Romper Room* because he was too disruptive.

Mr. Rogers's mom knitted many of the sweaters he wore on the air.

Nic Cage had two teeth extracted in preparation for his role in the 1984 movie *Birdy* to experience the pain his character would go through. He also slashed his arm for

Racing with the Moon (1984) and swallowed a cockroach for *Vampire's Kiss* (1992).

Katie Holmes is terrified of mice, raccoons, and public restrooms.

David Duchovny is a former vegetarian and is presently a pescatarian—one who eats fish, eggs, and dairy, but no meat.

Jennifer Aniston has the name of her dead dog Norman tattooed on her foot.

Twins Ashley and Mary-Kate Olsen, who played the same character on the TV show *Full House*, had to wear false teeth because their teeth were falling out and coming back in at different times during the program's run.

Matt Damon used to break-dance in Harvard Square for extra money.

Lisa Kudrow has a degree in sociobiology and did research on headaches before becoming famous.

Johnny Depp and Queen Elizabeth are distant cousins, twenty times removed.

Betty White has received twenty Emmy nominations during her career and won seven.

Betty White is the oldest person, at eighty-nine, to have hosted *Saturday Night Live*.

Alec Baldwin has guest-hosted *Saturday Night Live* a record sixteen times.

> Florence Henderson confided that she got crabs from a one-night stand with former New York mayor John Lindsay.

Richard Gere was offered a gymnastics scholarship from the University of Massachusetts.

> Elizabeth Taylor divorced her first husband by the time she was eighteen.

Alicia Keys played one of Rudy's friends on *The Cosby Show.*

> In the 1980s, under the name "Rus-le-Roq," Russell Crowe recorded a song called "I Want to Be Like Marlon Brando."

In 1991, Justin Timberlake, age ten, won the Pre-Teen Mr. America Pageant.

> Whitney Houston once sang the jingle for a Bounce fabric softener commercial.

Matthew Perry lost part of his middle finger in a nursery school accident.

> Sean Connery started going bald at twenty-one and wore a hairpiece for most of his films.

Paul Newman taught Jake Gyllenhaal how to parallel park for his driving test.

Jack Nicholson was raised by his grandparents and thought his mother, June, was his sister. He didn't find out the truth until a *Time* magazine reporter did an investigation in 1974 and exposed the lie.

DANGEROUS BEAUTY

Heidi Klum is the most dangerous celebrity to search for on the web. One in every ten online searches for Klum result in a website that tested positive for spyware, adware, spam, phishing, viruses, and other malware. The next four most dangerous celebs to "Google" are Cameron Diaz, Piers Morgan, Jessica Biel, and Katherine Heigl.

BAD ADS

Many American stars go to Japan to make big bucks doing cheesy television commercials that they would be too embarrassed to do in the United States. Several of the ads feature the star speaking Japanese, or dubbed doing so. A few notably funny examples follow (all are available for viewing on YouTube):

Michael J. Fox did a liquor commercial as a ninja-esque gardener, hopping about with hedge clippers and creating a topiary, while being chased around a mansion by a fat maid.

Nic Cage did an ad for a pachinko company while dressed up in a tacky cowboy outfit and head-butting other people dressed up like silver pachinko balls.

Brad Pitt shadowboxed, danced, put a wastebasket over his head, and smelled his armpits in an empty office to promote a coffee-in-a-can product.

John Travolta did a music video–like commercial where he worked out in a gym full of hot girls while plugging something called Tokyo Drink.

Ben Stiller hawked a drink called Chu-hi as a football player with a bunch of cheerleaders. (They don't play football in Japan.)

Arnold Schwarzenegger did an ad dressed in a golden toga for a drink called V&V.

Sylvester Stallone did a commercial playing golf, where suddenly a sausage on a fork appears from nowhere, which makes him very happy.

Natalie Portman did a Lux shampoo ad where she races on a motorcycle because she is late for her fencing audition. Her wonderful hair and fencing skills win her the job.

Hulk Hogan sang to a baby while dressed only in a diaper-type loincloth for a product called Big Flow air conditioners.

TWEETS FROM TWITS

The following are actual tweets from well-known celebrities:

Paris Hilton: "No, no, I didn't go to England. I went to London."

Jessica Biel: "I work out every day—Monday to Saturday."

Mary J. Blige: "Why is it that people always try to underestimate my intelligents?! They should never do that."

Ashton Kutcher: "Watching these dictated countries implode is just crushing."

50 Cent: "I can't believe my grandmother's making me take out the garbage. I'm rich! F**K this, I'm going home. I don't need this sh*t."

THE D-LIST

Steve Carell's first movie role was as a forty-five-second walk-on in the 1991 film *Curly Sue*.

Robert De Niro's first movie was 1968's *Greetings*, which was also the first movie to receive an X rating in the United States.

Ben Affleck played some kid on the street in 1981's *The Dark Side of the Street*.

Matt Damon had one line in the 1988 movie *Mystic Pizza*.

Demi Moore was in the 1982 horror flick *Parasite*.

Brad Pitt went uncredited in four 1987 films, including *Hunk* and *No Way Out*.

Leonardo DiCaprio had a guest spot on the TV show *Growing Pains* and his first film role was in 1991's *Critters 3*.

Jennifer Aniston was in the 1993 slasher flick *Leprechaun*.

Julia Roberts had two lines in her first movie, *Blood Red*, in 1987. Her brother Eric was also in the film.

Bruce Willis had three bit parts in early eighties movies, including a guy walking into a diner in *The First Deadly Sin* and a courtroom observer in *The Verdict*.

Michael Douglas was uncredited in 1966's *Cast a Long Shadow*.

LOOKING UP TO YOU

Many celebrity couples are not evenly matched in height. For example:

Jada is five feet and husband Will Smith is six foot two.

Seth Green is five foot four and wife Clare Grant is five foot seven.

Isla Fisher is five foot three and husband Sacha Baron Cohen is six foot three.

Mick Jagger is five foot ten and girlfriend L'Wren Scott is six foot four.

Fergie is five foot two and husband Josh Duhamel is six foot three.

Tom Cruise is five foot six and wife Katie Holmes is five foot nine. His ex-wife, Nicole Kidman, was even taller at five foot eleven.

LIKE A VIRGIN

Lisa Kudrow remained a virgin until she married at age thirty-two.

Virgin Jordin Sparks brings along a governess when she travels to help her resist temptation.

Carrie Underwood remained chaste until she married hockey player Mike Fisher in 2010.

Other gals who claim they remained "pure" until their wedding day include Jessica Simpson, Adriana Lima, Heidi Montag, and Hilary Duff.

BRAINIACS

Funnyman Conan O'Brien was the valedictorian of his high school class and later graduated magna cum laude from Harvard.

Jodie Foster graduated magna cum laude from Yale.

Brooke Shields has a degree in French literature from Princeton.

Actor James Woods scored a 1580 out of 1600 on his SATs.

Henry Winkler, aka the Fonz, got a master of fine arts degree from Yale.

TAT WAS A MISTAKE

Paris Hilton had boyfriend Nick Carter's name inked on her tush. Seven months later he was gone and so was the tattoo.

SLUM DOGHOUSE

Rubina Ali, who played the younger version of Latika in the movie *Slumdog Millionaire*, hardly became a millionaire herself for her Screen Actors Guild Award–winning role. She was paid five hundred pounds and promised a trust fund of an undisclosed amount if she continued her education after the age of eighteen. In March 2011, Ali's shanty in Mumbai burned down, along with her awards and memorabilia from the film, leaving her homeless.

HOP TO IT

Several famous women got their starts as *Playboy* bunnies, such as Deborah Harry of Blondie, who was a brunette at the time; Gloria Steinem, who had the job while researching an exposé for *Show* magazine; actress Lauren Hutton; Jacklyn Zeman, who played nurse Bobbie Spencer on *General Hospital*; and U.S. federal judge Kimba Wood.

THE DONALD

Donald Trump's grandfather was named Frederick Drumpf.

Trump is not a self-made millionaire, but is the son of a real estate tycoon.

Trump picked up the nickname "The Donald" after his Czechoslovakian wife Ivana referred to him as such in an interview.

Trump's most recent wife, as of 2011, is Slovenian Melania Knauss, twenty-four years his junior.

PRUDENT PITCHMAN

William Shatner may well be a billionaire—not from the *Star Trek* franchise, but from Priceline commercials. Shatner wisely opted to be paid in company stock for serving as their pitchman. The shares, which once sold for as little as two dollars, soared to close to five hundred dollars in early 2011.

EXES

These famous folks used to be couples:

Winona Ryder and Matt Damon

Lisa Kudrow and Conan O'Brien

Sienna Miller and P. Diddy

Drew Barrymore and Tom Green

Ashton Kutcher and January Jones

Ted Danson and Whoopi Goldberg

Nick Lachey and Kim Kardashian

Brad Pitt and Juliette Lewis

Demi Moore and Emilio Estevez

CELEBRITY ALIAS

Many celebs use aliases when checking into hotels or making other reservations. They often have fun with assumed names. Here is a list of stars and their aliases:

Mandy Moore: Meryl Lynch and Cornish Gamehen

Marilyn Monroe: Zelda Zonk

Brad Pitt and Jennifer Aniston: Mr. and Mrs. Ross Vegas, and Bruce and Jasmine Pilaf

Ozzy Osbourne: Prince Albert, Harry Bollocks ("bollocks" is British slang for testicles)

Slash: I. P. Freely

Deion Sanders: Rich Blackman

Elton John: Bobo Latrine, Brian Bigbum, and Sir Humphrey Handbag

Johnny Depp: Drip Noodle, Mr. Stench, and Mr. OddPong

Paul McCartney: Apple C. Vermouth

Chris Rock: Slappy White (an early black comedian)

Matt Damon: Matthew Carlsson-Page (his mother's maiden name) and John President

Kevin Costner: Frank Farmer

Tiger Woods: B. Simpson

John Travolta: J. T. Smith

Britney Spears: Alotta Warmheart

THAT'S NOT MY NAME

Joy Behar was born Josephina Victoria Occhiuto.

Tony Danza was christened Anthony Salvatore Iadanza.

Olivia Wilde used to be Olivia Jane Cockburn.

Sasha Alexander's given name is Suzana Drobnjakovic.

Lauren Bacall's old name was Betty Joan Perske.

YOU MUST BE KIDDING

Many celebrities come up with some rather interesting names for their kids, such as:

Kate Capshaw's daughter is named Destry Allyn.

Tommy Lee Jones's kid is Kafka.

Chef Jamie Oliver has three girls, named Poppy Honey Rosie, Daisy Boo Pamela, and Petal Blossom Rainbow.

Nicole Richie's son's name is Sparrow James Midnight.

Alicia Silverstone has a boy named Bear Blu.

Jennifer Connelly's brood are named Stellan, Kai, and Agnes Lark.

Natalie Portman's son is named Alef, after the first letter in the Hebrew alphabet.

Mariah Carey named her baby Moroccan Scott Cannon.

Kim Zolciak of *The Real Housewives of Atlanta* has a child named Kroy Jagger.

Volleyball player Kerri Walsh has a son named Sundance.

ACT YOUR AGE

Amanda Bynes played a teen in the movie *Easy A* when she was twenty-five.

Michael Trevino played teenager Tyler Lockwood in *The Vampire Diaries* when he was twenty-six.

Rachel McAdams was twenty-six when she played high school student Regina George in *Mean Girls*.

Shannon Elizabeth, who played the hot Czech exchange student in *American Pie*, was twenty-six at the time.

Tobey Maguire played teen Peter Parker in *Spider-Man* when he was twenty-seven.

Matthew Scott Parker was also twenty-seven when he played quarterback Jason Street on *Friday Night Lights*.

Keiko Agena played a sixteen-year-old on *Gilmore Girls* at age twenty-seven.

Jennifer Grey was twenty-seven when she played seventeen-year-old Baby in *Dirty Dancing*.

Cory Monteith led the club in *Glee* at twenty-eight.

Gabrielle Carteris played Andrea Zuckerman on *90210* at twenty-nine.

Trevor Donovan played Teddy Montgomery on *90210* at thirty-two.

Scott Wolf played Bailey Salinger on *Party of Five* at thirty-two.

GIRL TALK

Georgia native Nancy Grace decided to become a lawyer after the 1979 murder of her fiancé when she was nineteen. Grace served for ten years as a special prosecutor in the Atlanta-Fulton County district attorney's office, specializing in murder, rape, and child molestation cases.

Jane Velez-Mitchell, the award-winning journalist who hosts HLN's *Issues with Jane Velez-Mitchell*, was born to a Puerto Rican mother and an Irish American father and is a vegan.

WHAT'S COOKIN'?

Emeril Lagasse won a scholarship to the New England Conservatory of Music to play drums, but chose to pursue a career as a chef instead.

Giada De Laurentiis was born in Rome, Italy, and her grandfather was film producer Dino De Laurentiis.

Rachael Ray's middle name is Dominica.

Anthony Bourdain is six feet, four inches tall.

🌰 WOULD YOU LIKE MAALOX WITH THAT?

Andrew Zimmern, host of the television show *Bizarre Foods with Andrew Zimmern*, once was homeless for a year due to an alcohol and drug addiction. He survived by stealing purses and selling the contents.

Zimmern has eaten his share of disgusting foods on his program, including bull rectum and testicle soup, cod sperm chowder, chicken uterus, pit viper ice cream, wasp larvae, stinging nettle soup, live sea squirt, raw horse mane, jellied moose nose, frog ovary soup, and the still beating hearts of cobras, frogs, and tuna.

IT'S A DIRTY JOB

Dirty Jobs host Mike Rowe was an Eagle Scout and a stutterer.

Rowe sang professionally with the Baltimore Opera.

RUNWAY RINGLEADER

Project Runway designer supervisor Tim Gunn was a champion swimmer in high school.

At age seventeen, Gunn attempted suicide by swallowing about one hundred pills.

Gunn is openly asexual, claiming that he hasn't had a relationship since the early eighties.

Gunn is the chief creative officer for Liz Claiborne.

PSYCHOBABBLER

Dr. Phil McGraw played middle linebacker on the University of Tulsa football team. While he was anchoring their defense, the team suffered one of the worst losses in the history of college football, losing 100–6 to the University of Houston in 1968.

McGraw's PhD thesis was titled "Rheumatoid Arthritis: A Psychological Intervention."

Early in his career, McGraw was reprimanded and fined by the Texas State Board of Examiners of Psychologists for hiring an active patient to do part-time work for him.

McGraw started a trial consulting firm in 1990 that helped prepare Oprah Winfrey's defense in a libel lawsuit brought against her by Texas beef producers after she made disparaging comments about beef on her show during the mad cow disease scare.

In 2003, McGraw was threatened with an investigation by the Federal Trade Commission when he began marketing and selling his own line of weight-loss products on his TV show, even though he is not a clinical nutritionist.

McGraw's family members gave glowing testimonials that may have been overstated or misleading. The investigation was dropped after McGraw dissolved the business.

Dr. Phil married his first wife at the age of twenty and had the marriage annulled three years later.

McGraw's son, Jay, married Erica Dahm—one of the December 1998 *Playboy* Playmate triplets. Even though he is antipornography, Phil served as best man.

Presently, Dr. Phil makes about $30 million a year.

VIEWER'S CHOICE

The View cohost Joy Behar used to teach high school English on Long Island, New York.

Behar used to refer to her longtime boyfriend, Steve Janowitz, as her "spousal equivalent," before marrying him in 2011.

The View cohost Elisabeth Hasselback was a contestant on *Survivor: The Australian Outback* in 2001.

Hasselback was born Elisabeth DelPadre Filarski.

Hasselback was the captain of her Boston College softball team and worked for the Puma shoes design team after graduation.

Hasselback married former NFL quarterback Tim Hasselback in 2002.

In 2010, Hasselback became a spokesperson for Pro-Form's Ab Glider, an at-home stomach-toning device.

NO SPIN

Bill O'Reilly played semiprofessional baseball as a pitcher for the New York Monarchs.

O'Reilly was a classmate of Howard Stern while attending Boston University.

O'Reilly knew Billy Joel when the two were growing up on Long Island and has since referred to him as a "hood."

In 2004, former *The O'Reilly Factor* producer Andrea Mackris sued O'Reilly for $60 million for sexual harassment, claiming that he told her about his sexual fantasies involving her. He had sued her earlier on the same day, claiming extortion. O'Reilly and Mackris reached an undisclosed out-of-court settlement.

GET 'ER DONE

Daniel Lawrence Whitney, aka Larry the Cable Guy, was raised on a pig farm in Nebraska.

Larry the Cable Guy's fake southern accent is modeled after his college roommates, who were from Georgia and Texas.

TATER SALAD

Comedian Ron White picked up his nickname "Tater Salad" after serving in the navy and being kidded about his fondness for potato salad.

White maintains there is real Scotch in the glass he drinks from during his comedy shows.

White has a medicinal marijuana license, issued in California.

FOXXY

Jamie Foxx was born Eric Marion Bishop. He adopted his stage name when he realized that during open-mike comedy nights at clubs, female comedians were usually called to the stage first. His name is also a tribute to comedian Redd Foxx.

MARATHON MAN

Jerry Lewis began hosting the annual twenty-one-and-a-half-hour Muscular Dystrophy Association Telethon in 1966. He retired in 2011. In that time, the charity raised $1 billion.

NOTABLE NUPTIALS

The wedding of Michael Douglas to Catherine Zeta-Jones in 2005 featured invitations written in invisible ink and holograms. The event was held at New York's Plaza Hotel. The bride's diamond tiara cost $300,000 and her

Christian Lacroix gown went for $140,000. The whole shebang cost $1.5 million.

The wedding of Tom Cruise to Katie Holmes in 2006 took place in a fifteenth-century castle in Italy. The wedding cost $2 million and included guests' airfares of $900,000 and $180,000 worth of wine.

The wedding of Elizabeth Hurley to Arun Nayar in 2007 cost $2 million and took place over two days at two locations—Suderly Castle in England and Umaid Bhawan Palace in India. The couple paid $300,000 for private jets for the guests and $100,000 for accommodations.

Elizabeth Taylor's 1991 wedding to construction worker Larry Fortensky took place at Michael Jackson's Neverland Ranch and featured Jackson "giving away" Taylor. The extravaganza cost $2.5 million.

When Liza Minnelli married music producer David Gest in 2002, Michael Jackson was best man and Elizabeth Taylor was maid of honor. The $3.5 million wedding featured a sixty-piece orchestra, a $40,000 cake, and $700,000 in flowers.

Prince William's $34 million 2011 wedding to Kate Middleton featured $800,000 worth of flowers and an $80,000 cake.

The wedding of Paul McCartney to Heather Mills in 2002 cost $3.6 million, with $145,000 worth of flowers and a $150,000 fireworks display.

The wedding of Prince Charles to Diana Spencer in 1981 was the most expensive ever, at an inflation-adjusted cost of $110 million. There were twenty-seven cakes and a five-foot-tall main cake. A duplicate was made, just in case.

Chelsea Clinton's $5 million 2010 wedding to investment banker Marc Mezvinsky had $660,000 worth of air-conditioned tents.

Donald Trump had one hundred limos transport the guests for his 2005 wedding to Melania Knauss from the church to his $42 million mansion.

TV LAND

JUDY, JUDY, JUDY

In 2011, *Judge Judy*, starring Judy Sheindlin, was the most-watched daytime television show in America and the number one syndicated show.

Sheindlin is a retired New York family court judge.

As in most small-claims courts, monetary awards on the *Judge Judy* show are limited to five thousand dollars. The show's producers pay out the awards to the winning party. About 40 percent of the cases involve cash judgments.

Both plaintiffs and defendants receive one hundred dollars for appearing on the show, as well as thirty-five dollars a day and expenses for such things as airfare and hotels.

Judy serves as an arbitrator for the litigants appearing on the show. The parties must sign a waiver accepting Judy's ruling and agree not to pursue their cases any further elsewhere.

Although the program shows various scenes from New York City when they return from commercial breaks and a New York State flag can be seen behind the bench, *Judge Judy* is taped in Los Angeles.

WAY TO GO, JOE

The Jolly Joe Timmer Polka Show, based in Bethlehem, Pennsylvania, is the longest-running local-origination cable TV show in history.

DUNDER HEADS

The Office was a British TV comedy series before it was appropriated by Hollywood.

The main character, Michael, who was the boss at Dunder Mifflin, kept a Union Jack on his desk as a tribute to the show's English roots.

Rainn Wilson, who plays Dwight, auditioned for the part of Michael. Paul Giamatti and Martin Short were also considered for the role.

Steve Carell, who played Michael, used to be a correspondent on *The Daily Show*.

The cast drinks Crystal Club soda, a local Scranton, Pennsylvania, beverage, on the show.

The Office has never been rated higher than number fifty-two in the Nielsen ratings.

WHAT'S THE DEAL

Deal or No Deal was adapted from a 2002 Dutch show.

The total amount of all the money in the twenty-six cases on *Deal or No Deal* adds up to $3,418,416.01.

POTTY MOUTHS

South Park holds the Guinness record for most swear words used in an animated series.

South Park was the first weekly TV show to be assigned the TV-MA rating.

Cocreator Matt Stone does the voice for Kenny by speaking into his sleeve.

The character Chef was inspired by a food hall worker at the University of Colorado, where cocreators Matt Stone and Trey Parker went to school.

Mr. Hankey (a piece of feces) was inspired by Trey Parker's father, who warned him that his poop would rise up and eat him if he didn't flush the toilet.

Cartman's promiscuous mother is named Liane, after Parker's ex-fiancée, whom he caught cheating on him.

Cartman's full name is Eric Theodore Cartman.

SPONGE-WORTHY

SpongeBob SquarePants was originally named Sponge-Boy, but that name was already trademarked.

> SpongeBob's creator, Stephen Hillenburg, was a marine biologist. He brought a fish tank with him to the Nickelodeon offices to help sell his idea for the show to the network execs. Hillenburg was also a director of *Rocko's Modern Life*.

Patrick's last name is Star.

TEENAGE WASTELAND

The working titles for *That '70s Show* were "Teenage Wasteland" and "The Kids Are Alright," both songs by the Who.

> The show's directors used a rotating camera to depict the teen characters getting high in the basement, without ever showing them actually smoking marijuana.

Fes(z) stands for "foreign exchange student." His country of origin is never mentioned.

> Mila Kunis, who plays an American, Jackie, was born in what is today Ukraine. Wilmer Valderrama, who plays foreigner Fez, was born in America.

All episode titles for season five were Led Zeppelin songs, for season six Who songs, for season seven Rolling Stones songs, and for season eight Queen songs.

Laura Prepon, who played Donna, went from being a redhead to a blonde for the last two seasons because she had to bleach her hair for a movie role she had played.

IT'S WORTH HOW MUCH?

Tickets for *Antiques Roadshow* are free. People are pre-selected at random to attend.

Antiques Roadshow is based on a similar 1979 British appraisal show.

The highest appraisal ever on the show was $1.5 million in 2011 for Chinese bowls carved from rhinoceros horns. They bested the previous record holder, $1.07 million for Chinese jade and celadon pieces that later sold at auction for $494,615.

Other top appraisals include a 1937 Clyfford Still oil painting for $500,000 and a Ute chief's blanket for between $300,000 and $500,000.

TAXI TRIVIA

Like many other American TV programs, *Cash Cab* was originally a British show.

There is no cash in the *Cash Cab*. Winners are sent a check in the mail.

Some *Cash Cab* contestants are preselected.

U.S. host Ben Bailey is a licensed New York City cabbie.

THE BRITISH ARE COMING

All in the Family was not created by Norman Lear, as is commonly believed. It was originally a British TV show created by Johnny Speight, called *Till Death Us Do Part*. The main character was called Alf Garnett, not Archie Bunker.

Several other successful American TV shows are British television remakes, including *Airline, American Gladiators, American Idol, Cosby, Dancing with the Stars, Dear John, Hell's Kitchen, It's Me or the Dog, Kitchen Nightmares, Men Behaving Badly, Not Necessarily the News, Sanford and Son, Supernanny, Three's Company, Too Close for Comfort, Trading Spaces, Undercover Boss, What Not to Wear, Whose Line Is It Anyway?, Who Wants to Be a Millionaire, Wife Swap/Trading Spouses,* and *The X Factor*.

HIT PARADE

TWAIN'S WORLD

Shania Twain is the top female country singer of all time. Her 1997 *Come On Over* is the bestselling album by a woman of any genre, and the bestselling country album in history.

Twain used to clean the house of her singing coach in exchange for his services.

In 1987, Twain's mother and stepfather died in a car accident and she moved home to take care of her siblings.

In 1993, Twain married rock producer Robert "Mutt" Lange. They divorced in 2010, after she discovered that he was having an affair with her best friend, Marie-Anne Thiebaud. Twain took her revenge by marrying Thiebaud's ex-husband in 2011.

Twain originally wanted to be a rock singer.

PRECOCIOUS PERFORMER

LeAnn Rimes was the youngest Grammy winner ever, taking home the award for Best New Artist at age fourteen.

In 2000, Rimes sued her father and her former manager to recover $7 million she alleged they had stolen from her in the previous five years. She settled with them for an undisclosed amount in 2002.

CARRIE COUNTRY

Carrie Underwood is the bestselling *American Idol* winner, surpassing Kelly Clarkson in 2011.

Underwood grew up in Oklahoma and graduated salutatorian from her high school.

Underwood was voted "World's Sexiest Vegetarian" by PETA (People for the Ethical Treatment of Animals) in 2007.

Underwood dated NFL quarterback Tony Romo in 2007 and married NHL star Mike Fisher in 2010.

COUNTRY COUPLES

Kenny Chesney married actress Renée Zellweger in 2005. The marriage was annulled four months later.

Country singer Vince Gill is married to Christian pop singer Amy Grant.

Martina McBride's husband was a concert production manager for Garth Brooks and she sold Brooks's souvenirs. Brooks offered her a chance to become his opening act after becoming impressed with her.

Samuel Timothy "Tim" McGraw is married to fellow country music star Faith Hill and is the son of former Major League Baseball pitcher Tug McGraw.

McGraw grew up believing his stepfather was his real father and that he had the last name of Smith, until he accidentally found his birth certificate at age eleven. Tug McGraw, however, would not acknowledge Tim as his son for another seven years.

McGraw's Soul2Soul II Tour 2006 with Faith Hill was the highest-grossing tour in country music history.

Faith Hill was adopted as an infant.

Hill sang to inmates at a Mississippi prison in her youth, before moving to Nashville and selling T-shirts.

Hill was discovered one day while singing to herself at her job as a secretary at a music publishing company.

PARTY ON GARTH

Troyal Garth Brooks has sold the most albums in the United States since 1991 and is the second-bestselling album artist of all time in the United States, behind only Elvis Presley.

Brooks threw the javelin for the Oklahoma State University track team.

In 2000, Brooks wanted to donate part of his liver to fellow country musician Chris LeDoux, but was not a compatible match.

Brooks married Patricia "Trisha" Lynn Yearwood in 2005. She got her big break in music when she sang backing vocals on Brooks's hugely successful album *No Fences*. She was soon the opening act on Brooks's next tour.

FROM THE BOTTOM UP

Alan Eugene Jackson began his music career in the mail room of the Nashville Network.

HOLEY MUSIC

Willie Nelson's guitar is named Trigger after Roy Rogers's horse. He acquired the Martin N-20 nylon-string instrument in 1969 and has played it ever since. Because it was made as a classical guitar, it has no pick guard, and Nelson's vigorous pick playing has opened a gaping hole in the body just below the strings.

JERSEY BOYS AND GIRLS

Country star Clint Black was born "down the shore," in Long Branch, New Jersey.

While trying to make it in the music business, Black supported himself by cutting bait, being a fishing guide, and doing construction.

Country songstress Mary Chapin Carpenter was born in Princeton, New Jersey.

CITY SLICKER

Roy Clark grew up in Staten Island, New York, and Washington, DC.

URBAN COWBOY

Keith Lionel Urbanski was born in New Zealand and got started in the Australian country music business.

Urban dated model Niki Taylor before marrying Nicole Kidman.

Urban sued a New Jersey painter with the same name who had the website KeithUrban.com. The singer lost to the painter in court.

NOBODY'S PATSY

Patsy Cline, born Virginia Patterson Hensley, suffered a throat infection when she was a child that she credits with giving her "a voice that boomed like Kate Smith's."

Cline was the first female country singer to perform at Carnegie Hall.

Cline died in a plane crash in Tennessee in 1963.

PARDON ME

Merle Haggard was sent to juvenile detention centers four times as a youth, escaping from two of them. He was later arrested for robbing a liquor store and sent to San Quentin Prison. Haggard was pardoned by Governor Ronald Reagan in 1972.

Haggard has been married five times.

JONESING FOR A DRINK

George Jones is known as "the Possum" because of his distinctive nose and other facial features.

Jones was a notorious drinker. Once, after his wife Tammy Wynette hid all the car keys, he hopped on his lawn mower and drove it down the highway to the nearest bar, ten miles away.

Jones has been married four times.

WELL-OILED PERFORMER

Toby Keith Covel played semiprofessional football for the Oklahoma City Drillers and worked on the oil fields before making it big in music.

Keith didn't get his break in the business until he was thirty-three, when a flight attendant who was a fan gave a demo tape of Keith's to a Mercury Records exec on a flight she was working and he loved it.

COAL MINER'S DAUGHTER

Loretta Lynn was born Loretta Webb and was named for actress Loretta Young.

Crystal Gayle is Lynn's sister.

Although Lynn's husband was a chronic philanderer, they stayed married for fifty years.

REALLY REBA

Reba Nell McEntire is the second-bestselling female country artist, after Shania Twain.

McEntire's father was World Champion Steer Roper three times.

BUCK UP

At the age of three or four, Alvis Edgar Owens Jr. walked into his family's Texas home and announced that from then on he wanted to be called "Buck." And he was.

Owens was married four times.

PITCHING PRIDE

Charlie Pride was a pitcher for the Memphis Red Sox of the old Negro American League and worked his way up to a Class C team of the New York Yankees before an injury ended his career.

For the first two years of his country music career, there were no pictures of Pride distributed with his records, to avoid his songs being banned from airplay because he was black.

Pride is a part owner of the Texas Rangers baseball team.

STRAIT DOPE

George Harvey Strait holds the record for most number one singles in any genre of music—fifty-seven.

Strait's thirteen-year-old daughter, Jenifer, was killed in a car crash in 1986.

Strait drives Chevys and refers to them in his songs.

TUCKER TIME

Tanya Tucker had her first hit song, "Delta Dawn," at age thirteen.

Tucker had relationships with Andy Gibb, Merle Haggard, Don Johnson, and Glen Campbell.

ALL ATWITTER

Conway Twitty, born Harold Lloyd Jenkins, is second only to George Strait, with fifty-five number one *Billboard* country hit songs.

Twitty was offered a chance to play baseball by the Philadelphia Phillies after high school, but was drafted into the army.

ARE YOU READY FOR SOME FOOTBALL?

Hank Williams Jr., who sang the opening songs for *Monday Night Football*, is the son of country music legend Hank Williams.

Hank Williams Jr. had a near-fatal fall down a 442-foot cliff while climbing Ajax Mountain, Montana, in 1975. He required two years of reconstructive surgeries and therapies and had to learn to speak again.

IDOL THOUGHTS

Randy Jackson, a judge on *American Idol*, once played bass guitar for Jerry Garcia, Journey, Bruce Springsteen, Madonna, Bob Dylan, Jon Bon Jovi, Billy Joel, Mariah Carey, Carlos Santana, and many others, before becoming a producer of records.

In 2003, Randy Jackson lost 114 pounds after having gastric bypass surgery.

Former *American Idol* judge Paula Abdul was a cheerleader for the Los Angeles Lakers in the 1980s.

Abdul is tied for fifth among female artists to reach number one on the *Billboard* Hot 100 chart, which she did six times.

Abdul's father was a Syrian Jew. Her mother was a Canadian Jew.

> Abdul was discovered by the Jacksons, who saw her perform as a Laker Girl and hired her to choreograph their videos and tours.

Abdul choreographed Tom Hanks's famous keyboard dancing scene in the movie *Big*.

> Abdul was married to actor Emilio Estevez from 1992 to 1994.

In 2004, Abdul was convicted of a misdemeanor hit-and-run accident on an L.A. freeway.

> Abdul claims to suffer from complex regional pain syndrome, a chronic progressive disease causing swelling and pain in the skin.

DIVA DISH

Pink (P!nk) was born Alecia Beth Moore. Her stage name is a tribute to the character "Pink" in the film *Reservoir Dogs*.

> *Billboard* rated Pink as the number one Pop Song Artist of the Decade (2000–2009).

Pink proposed to her future husband, motocross racer Carey Hart, by holding up a "Will you marry me?" sign during one of his races. The couple has a daughter named Willow Sage Hart.

Robyn Rihanna Fenty, better known as Rihanna, was born in Barbados and moved to America at age sixteen to pursue a career in music.

Since 2005, Rihanna has had the most number one singles on the *Billboard* Hot 100—ten.

Gwen Renée Stefani was named after a stewardess in the 1968 novel *Airport.* Her middle name is from the song "Don't Walk Away Renée."

Stefani competed on her high school swim team in an effort to lose weight. She also worked at a Dairy Queen during this time.

Adele Laurie Blue Adkins is known professionally as just "Adele."

Christina Aguilera first came to prominence when she appeared on the *Star Search* talent TV show, where she finished second, in 1990. She then went on to star on Disney's *All New Mickey Mouse Club* from 1993 to 1994.

Kelly Clarkson wanted to be a marine biologist when she was young, but after watching the movie *Jaws,* she had a change of heart.

Eleven of Fergie's singles have been downloaded more than 2 million times each—the most of any artist.

When Fergie was nine she did voice-over work as the character Sally in *Peanuts* cartoons and she was also a spelling bee champion.

Amy Winehouse is the only female British singer to have won five Grammy awards.

> Winehouse, who died in 2011, had a hit song titled "Rehab," where she sang about refusing to enter drug rehabilitation. She is reported to have died from alcohol poisoning.

Winehouse had been arrested multiple times for common assault and is rumored to have spit upon Pippa Middleton, sister of the Duchess of Cornwall, during one fracas.

LOOSE CHANGE

Curtis James Jackson III, better known as 50 Cent, was a crack dealer when he was twelve.

> Jackson's mother, Sabrina, who was a cocaine dealer, had him when she was fifteen. She was murdered when he was twelve.

After serving time at a correctional boot camp, Jackson changed his name to "50 Cent" to signify the "change" in his life.

> In 2000, 50 Cent was shot nine times while sitting in the back of a car. The alleged assailant, one of Mike Tyson's bodyguards—Darryl "Hommo" Baum—was killed three weeks later.

50 Cent was the second-richest rapper in 2007 and now lives in Mike Tyson's former mansion in Connecticut.

FROM RAPS TO RICHES

Rapper Shawn Corey Carter, better known as Jay-Z, is worth more than $450 million and is a part owner of the New Jersey Nets basketball team.

Carter's stage name is taken from the J/Z subway line that had a stop near his boyhood home in Brooklyn.

Jay-Z once shot his brother in the shoulder for stealing his jewelry.

When Jay-Z married Beyoncé in 2008, he bought her a $5 million wedding ring.

A LIL' TROUBLE

Female rapper Lil' Kim was sentenced to one year and one day in prison for lying to a grand jury about a shooting incident in 2001.

Rapper Lil Wayne accidentally shot himself with a 9mm handgun when he was thirteen. At age fourteen, although an honor student, he dropped out of school to pursue music.

Lil Wayne fathered his first child when he was fifteen.

In 2010, Wayne was sentenced to one year in prison for carrying a concealed weapon.

ABSOLUTELY LUDACRIS

Ludacris was born Christopher Brian Bridges.

Before rising to stardom as a rapper, Bridges interned as a radio DJ in Atlanta working under the name "Chris Lova Lova."

MR. BIG

Notorious B.I.G. was born Christopher George Latore Wallace, but picked up the nickname "Big" as a boy because of his size.

Big started selling drugs at age twelve.

Big went to the state-funded George Westinghouse Information Technology High School in Brooklyn that Jay-Z and Busta Rhymes attended.

When he was eighteen, Big spent nine months in prison for selling crack.

THUG LIFE

Tupac Amaru Shakur was named after Túpac Amaru II, a Peruvian revolutionary who led indigenous peoples against the Spanish and was later executed.

Both of Shakur's parents were Black Panthers.

In high school, Shakur played the part of the Mouse King in the school's presentation of *The Nutcracker*.

Shakur had the words "Thug Life" tattooed across his stomach.

Shakur's favorite writers were Sun Tzu, William Shakespeare, Kurt Vonnegut, and Machiavelli. (Shakur went by the nickname "Makaveli.")

Shakur is the bestselling hip-hop/rap artist of all time.

In 1992, Shakur had an argument with members of a crowd of autograph seekers. He pulled out a gun and cocked it, before it fell to the ground. Somebody picked it up and it discharged, killing a six-year-old boy some distance away. His record company settled with the boy's family for several hundred thousand dollars.

In 1994, Shakur was convicted of sexually abusing a woman. The day before he was convicted, Shakur was shot five times in Manhattan. In 1995, he became the only artist to have a number one album on the *Billboard* 200 while serving time in prison.

In 1996, Shakur and his entourage beat up a Crips gang member in Las Vegas, whom he was having an ongoing dispute with. Later that night, Shakur was killed in a drive-by shooting while a passenger in a BMW 750Li sedan. The murderer was never caught.

MAN OF MANY NAMES

Sean Combs habitually changes his name. So far, he has gone by Puff Daddy, Puffy, Puff, P. Diddy, Diddy, and

King Combs. In 2011, for one week, he wanted to be called "Swag," which he said was short for "swagger." His nickname "Puff" came from his "huffing and puffing" as a child when he got upset.

> With an estimated wealth of $475 million, Sean Combs was ranked by *Forbes* magazine in 2011 as the richest man in hip-hop.

In 1991, Combs promoted a concert event in the gymnasium of the City College of New York that he knowingly oversold by twice the gym's seating capacity. Once the gym was full, his people pushed a table against the only door to a stairwell leading into the gym, trapping the crush of people trying to enter. In the ensuing panic and stampede, nine concertgoers were killed. Combs was found 50 percent liable and the college security force was found 50 percent liable.

AW, HELL NO!

Willard Christopher "Will" Smith Jr. rapped under the name the Fresh Prince in the late 1980s.

> Smith is the only actor to ever have eight consecutive movies that grossed $100 million and the only actor to have eight consecutive movies debut number one at the box office.

Smith was the first hip-hop artist to be nominated for an Academy Award.

The catchphrase "Aw, hell no!" is incorporated into all Smith's movies.

A LITTLE TLC

The hip-hop trio TLC originally consisted of Lisa "Left Eye" Lopez, Rozonda "Chilli" Thomas, and Tionne "T-Boz" Watkins. TLC is an amalgamation of the names "T-Boz," "Left Eye," and "Chilli."

In 1994, Lopez set fire to the tennis shoes of her boyfriend, Andre Rison, the professional football player. The fire spread and burned down the mansion they shared. She was sentenced to five years probation and therapy.

Lopez died in a head-on collision while working to set up a school in Honduras in 2002.

Watkins has sickle-cell anemia and wasn't expected to live past her thirties. In 2006, she was diagnosed with a brain tumor that was successfully removed.

Thomas has a son named Tron.

STAGE HOG

Kanye West's father was a Black Panther.

West's mother died from complications related to breast augmentation surgery and a tummy tuck procedure. She was advised by her first plastic surgeon that she had a heart condition that would prevent her from being a candidate for these procedures, but she went to another doctor and had them done anyway, resulting in her death.

President Barack Obama called West a "jackass" after the infamous incident when West jumped up on stage at the 2009 MTV Video Music Awards and grabbed the microphone from singer Taylor Swift during her acceptance of an award, saying Beyoncé should have won instead.

CHURCH USHER

Usher sang in his church choir at the age of nine.

TOUR DE FORCE

U2's two-year 360 world stadium tour, which wrapped up in July 2011, is the highest-grossing concert tour of all time. It made more than $717 million and topped the previous record holder, the Rolling Stones' 2005–07 Bigger Bang tour, which raked in $455 million.

Sting did a 2009 concert at the behest of the daughter of brutal Uzbekistan dictator Islam Karimov for a reported 2 million British pounds.

On New Year's Eve 1994, Rod Stewart played at a free concert on Copacabana Beach in Rio de Janeiro that attracted 3.5 million spectators.

Elton John performed at Rush Limbaugh's fourth wedding for a fee of $1 million.

MUSIC MEN

Keith Richards plays a guitar with five strings.

AC/DC guitarist Angus Young goes into a trademark "spasm" while playing, where he falls to the floor, kicking, shaking, and spinning in circles, all the while continuing to play. He came up with this shtick during an early gig in Australia, when he accidentally tripped over a wire on stage and faked a spasm as if it were part of the act in order to avoid embarrassment.

Jersey rockers Bruce Springsteen and Jon Bon Jovi both get large tax breaks on some of their New Jersey estate properties by taking advantage of the state's liberal farm tax assessment program. Springsteen grows some organic vegetables and Bon Jovi keeps honeybees.

Van Halen used to rent PA equipment from David Lee Roth before he joined the band. They later decided it would be cheaper to just ask him to be their singer.

Eddie Van Halen had one-third of his tongue removed due to tongue cancer.

NOT THRILLED

Rolling Stone magazine named REM's *Murmur* album the best of 1983, ahead of Michael Jackson's *Thriller* and the Police's *Synchronicity*.

HEADBANGER

Jefferson Airplane changed their name to Starship because of member Paul Kantner's obsession with science fiction movies.

> Starship's drummer, Donny Baldwin, once beat singer Mickey Thomas so severely that he required surgery to reconstruct his face.

THANKS, MOM

In 2007, Justin Bieber's mother posted a video on YouTube of him singing in a local Stratford, Ontario, talent contest, which record producer Scooter Braun stumbled upon accidentally while searching for another singer. Braun showed the clip to Usher and the thirteen-year-old Bieber was signed to a record deal and became an overnight sensation.

> Bieber's mother initially resisted Braun's request to represent her son because he was Jewish.

In 2011, Bieber cut his iconic hair, a lock of which was auctioned off for $40,668. The rest of his hair clippings toured the United States and fans could get their picture taken with the hair for a small donation to charity.

FOR THE RECORD

Lady Gaga holds the Guinness record for most consecutive weeks on the United Kingdom singles charts, at 154.

Gaga also holds the record for Most-Searched-For Female on the Internet, beating out previous champ Sarah Palin.

Michael Jackson holds the Guinness record for Most-Searched-For Male on the Internet.

Michael Jackson's red "Thriller" jacket sold for $1.8 million in 2011.

NAME THAT BAND

Nickelback's name comes from the days when band member Mike Kroeger worked at a Starbucks and the countless times he told customers, "Here's your nickel back."

'N Sync got their name after Justin Timberlake's mother commented on how "in sync" the boys sounded.

I HAVE A GRAMMY

Martin Luther King Jr. won the Grammy Award for Best Spoken Word Recording in 1971 for "Why I Oppose the War in Vietnam."

THE KING OF SWING

Benny Goodman started the Big Band era when his *Let's Dance* radio program was first broadcast on national radio in 1934.

HOT HITS

Billboard magazine puts out more than one hundred music charts each week. The *Billboard* Hot 100 ranks the top singles and the *Billboard* 200 ranks the bestselling albums.

The first song to top the Hot 100, in 1958, was Ricky Nelson's "Poor Little Fool." There have been 1,003 top songs since then (at the time of this writing).

SMALL SCREEN, BIG HIT

Many television theme songs have gone on to become big hits, including:

"Welcome Back," performed by John Sebastian, from *Welcome Back, Kotter*, went to number one on the *Billboard* Hot 100 chart in 1976.

"How Do You Talk to an Angel," by the Heights, from *The Heights*, went to number one in 1992.

"I'll Be There for You," by the Rembrandts, from *Friends*, went to number one in 1995.

"The Theme from *Miami Vice*," by Jan Hammer, went to number one in 1985.

"Good Ol' Boys," by Waylon Jennings, from *The Dukes of Hazzard*, went to number one on the country charts in 1980.

"Believe It Or Not," by Joey Scarbury, from *The Greatest American Hero*, went to number two in 1981.

"Secret Agent Man," by Johnny Rivers, from *Secret Agent*, went to number three in 1964.

"The Theme from *Hawaii Five-O*," by the Ventures, made it to number four in 1969.

"Bad Boys (Theme from *Cops*)," by Inner Circle, went to number eight in 1993.

"The Theme from *Hill Street Blues*," by Mike Port, went to number ten in 1981.

"The Theme from *The Rockford Files*," by Mike Post, went to number ten in 1975 and remained on the *Billboard* charts for forty-four weeks.

The theme songs from *Batman*, *Bonanza*, *Baretta*, *Cheers*, *Dawson's Creek*, *Moonlighting*, *Magnum P.I.*, and *Laverne and Shirley* all were top twenty-five *Billboard* Hot 100 hits.

SCIENTIFIC NOTATION

REFLECT ON THIS

Earth reflects back into space about 35 percent of the energy reaching it from the sun.

POLE POSITION

Earth's North Magnetic Pole is presently situated under the Arctic Ocean near northern Canada.

The magnetic pole moves around due to currents in the earth's core. It is moving toward Siberia at a rate of thirty-five miles a year.

HOT ROCKS

Diamonds were formed 1 billion years ago at depths of one hundred miles beneath the earth's surface.

The diamonds being mined today were blasted to the surface at supersonic speeds during ancient volcanic eruptions.

About 130 million carats of diamonds are mined each year, with a total value of about $9 billion.

Diamonds can be found in Arkansas, Colorado, and Montana.

Astronomers have discovered a planet four thousand light-years away that they believe is made of extremely dense carbon. In other words, it may be a gigantic diamond.

Rubies and sapphires both are composed of aluminum oxide, or corundum, the only difference being color. All red or pink gem varieties of corundum are known as rubies, while all other colors, including blue, are considered sapphires.

The word "sapphire" comes from the Greek *sappheiros*, meaning "blue stone."

Sapphires are the second-hardest mineral, after diamonds.

BLACK GOLD

Crude oil is usually black or dark brown, but can emerge from the earth as yellowish, reddish, or greenish in color.

ALL WET

Each year the sea level rises 3.1 millimeters.

If the water from all of the world's oceans evaporated, the remaining salt, if collected, would form a cube 165 miles on each side.

About 6 million years ago, the Strait of Gibraltar closed together and the Mediterranean Sea completely evaporated, over a period of 1,000 years. After being dry for 170,000 years, the strait suddenly reopened and the Mediterranean basin filled with water again.

The fourth-largest ocean is the Southern Ocean, which extends north from the coast of Antarctica to 60° south latitude.

One gallon of water can produce 1 billion snowflakes.

THE BLOOP

In 1997, the National Atmospheric and Oceanographic Administration detected the loudest non-man-made oceanic sound ever, off the west coast of the tip of South America. The extremely powerful ultra-low-frequency underwater sound, which was nicknamed the "Bloop," could be heard five thousand kilometers away from its source. Scientists believe it was made by some living creature, but it was five times louder, and different, than any animal noise known to science.

MYSTERY RADIO

UVB-76 is a shortwave radio station in Russia that continuously broadcasts a series of short, beeping sounds at the rate of about twenty-five per minute and has been doing so since 1982. No one knows what the purpose of these transmissions is, but on rare occasions, voices can be heard in the background.

UN*SAND*ITARY

According to the Environmental Protection Agency, beach sand has been found to contain *E. coli*, and beach-goers are advised to wash their hands in fresh water before eating food on the beach.

POWER SURGE

The low pressure in the eye of a hurricane causes a suc-tion that creates a large mound of water. High winds push the mound onshore, resulting in a potentially deadly surge. Half of all U.S. hurricane deaths result from the storm surge.

HOT AND COLD

In 1980, Dallas, Texas, had a record forty-two consecu-tive days with temperatures above 100°F.

On February 11, 2011, it was colder in Bartlesville, Oklahoma, than it was at the South Pole at −28°F.

The temperature at the South Pole has never gone above freezing in recorded history.

The South Pole gets colder than the North Pole, because the South Pole is at an elevation of nine thousand feet, while the North Pole is close to sea level. Also, the South Pole is surrounded by ice-covered land, while the North Pole is surrounded by the Arctic Ocean, which moderates its temperature.

Due to the warming influence of the Gulf Stream, the coast of England is mild enough to support palm trees.

The temperature of any cave is equal to the average of the year-round temperature of the air outside.

QUIET ZONE

There is no noise in the upper atmosphere, since there are not enough air particles to carry sound waves.

POSITIVELY PLASMA

Plasma is a state of matter distinct from solid, liquid, and gas.

Plasma is a high-energy state of matter in which atomic nuclei and the electrons orbiting them separate, resulting in a collection of charged particles containing an equal number of positive ions and electrons.

Heating a gas can ionize its atoms, turning it into plasma.

Most of the ordinary matter in the universe is plasma, including all stars.

Lightning and auroras are made of plasma.

Fluorescent lights, neon signs, and plasma TVs all contain plasma.

SPOUTING OFF

Crater Lake in Oregon was formed seven thousand years ago when a volcano named Mazama blew its top, leaving a six-mile-wide caldera that filled with water.

Costa Rica and Guatemala each have five active volcanoes.

Alaska has seventeen active volcanoes.

BURN NOTICE

The color of fire is influenced by the amount of oxygen available. Low-oxygen fires burn yellow, while high-oxygen fires burn blue.

The reason a candle flame is blue at the bottom and yellow at the top is because it pulls in fresh air from the bottom and has less oxygen available farther up the flame.

Prehistoric humans were creating fire four hundred thousand years ago.

The Great Fire of London in 1666 not only destroyed 80 percent of the city, but also killed off the flea-infested rats that were spreading the plague throughout the city.

Pistachios contain oils that can spontaneously combust when they decompose.

DRY DATA

Technically, a desert is any area of land that gets less than ten inches of precipitation a year.

Dry ice is the solid form of carbon dioxide.

Dry ice does not melt into a liquid, but sublimates, going directly from a solid state to a gaseous state.

Dry ice is −110°F. Exposure to the skin for more than one second will cause frostbite.

HARD DATA

A mineral is comprised of one type of element or chemical substance. A rock, on the other hand, is comprised of more than one type of mineral.

The oldest known rocks on Earth are the 4.4-billion-year-old zircon crystals found in the Jack Hills of Western Australia.

The median radius of Earth is 3,958.8 miles.

There is a huge mountain range with nine-thousand-foot peaks under two miles of ice in Antarctica.

DROPPING ACID

The term "acid test" derives from the practice of placing a drop of nitric acid on gold to verify its authenticity. Nitric acid does not react with gold, but does so with most other metals.

IT'S ELEMENTARY

Eighteen-carat gold is 75 percent gold. Fourteen-carat gold is 58.3 percent gold.

> There are seventeen rare earth elements. Rare earth elements aren't really rare; they are just as abundant as lead and tin, but they are not concentrated and are difficult to extract.

China produces 97 percent of the world's rare earth supply.

> One rare earth element—neodymium—is used to make the world's strongest magnets, which are used in laptops and speakers.

I FEEL THE EARTH MOVE

The earthquake that devastated Japan in 2011 lifted and then dropped a slab of seafloor 50 miles wide by 180 miles long, shifting the seafloor eighty feet to the west.

> The tsunami that was triggered by the 2011 earthquake caused icebergs to break off of the Sulzberger Ice Shelf in Antarctica eight thousand miles away.

The 2011 quake in Japan also shortened Earth's day by 1.8 microseconds, by shifting the distribution of its mass, which caused it to spin a little faster.

The quake also shifted the tilt of Earth's axis by six inches.

The earthquake that wreaked havoc in Haiti in 2010 resulted when two of Earth's plates abruptly shifted laterally six feet, sending thirteen-foot ripple waves through the ground.

In 2011, the Italian government charged the country's top seismologist with manslaughter for failing to predict a 2009 earthquake that killed 308 people. According to the U.S. Geological Survey, no major earthquake has ever been successfully predicted.

WOBBLY WORLD

Earth's rotation changes all the time as a result of atmospheric winds and ocean currents.

The tilt of Earth's axis naturally changes by about 3.3 feet over the course of an average year.

THAT SUCKS

The vacuum created by a tornado can literally suck the air out of one's lungs.

SILVER LINING

Despite the direness of global warming, there are actually a few benefits to such a climate change, including:

Expanded warm areas in the northern climates, with plenty of moisture and carbon dioxide, will greatly increase food production.

There will be increased habitat for wildlife, and many species will flourish.

Fewer people will die from the contagious diseases that kill tens of thousands during the winter months.

Less energy will be consumed for heating in present-day cold climates.

Plus, the inevitable next ice age may be postponed.

THE DEEP SEEP

Radon comes from a natural breakdown of uranium in soil, rock, and water.

According to the EPA, radon is the second-leading cause of lung cancer in nonsmokers.

PLANETARIUM

The temperature on the equator of Mars can reach a balmy 70°F during the Martian summer.

The surface of Jupiter is 17,000°F, hotter than the surface of the sun.

Jupiter has an ocean of hydrogen, below which lies an ocean of helium.

MANY MOONS

The inner core of the moon is a solid iron alloy. The outer core is a liquid (molten) iron alloy.

Saturn's moon Titan has cryo-volcanoes that spew "lava" not of molten rock, but of a mixture of water and ammonia that freezes at −100°C.

At −179°C, Titan is so cold that all water is frozen, but there are lakes and rivers of liquid methane.

A GALAXY FAR, FAR AWAY

The predicted collision of the Andromeda and Milky Way spiral galaxies in 3 to 5 billion years will form a huge elliptical galaxy that astronomers refer to as Milkomeda.

The Milky Way galaxy makes about five new stars a year.

The two closest galaxies to the Milky Way were just discovered in the past several years. The Sagittarius dwarf galaxy was discovered in 1994 and contains about 1 billion stars. The Canis Major dwarf galaxy was discovered in 2003 and also has about 1 billion stars. This galaxy is closer to Earth than Earth is to the center of the Milky Way. These two galaxies are so close that they are currently colliding with the Milky Way galaxy. The reason these two dwarf galaxies were not found earlier is because they lie along the galactic plane and are hidden by stars, gas, and dust.

Galaxies are grouped together in the universe gravitationally, in long filaments. The universe is thus like a gigantic filamentous sponge with huge voids found between the boundaries of these filaments.

High-velocity stars are flung by the supermassive black hole at the center of the Milky Way galaxy with such force that they shoot right out of the galaxy into empty space.

The Sloan Great Wall is an enormous wall of galaxies and is the largest known structure in the universe, stretching some 1.37 billion light-years in length.

HEADS UP

Each year, forty thousand metric tons of space debris fall to Earth.

One Lottie Williams of Tulsa, Oklahoma, is the only known person to be hit by man-made space debris falling to Earth. In 1997, she was hit with a piece of fiberglass mesh insulation from a U.S. Air Force Delta II rocket fuel tank that was launched a year earlier. Happily, the small five-inch piece was very light and she was not injured.

TINY TALES

Thousands of mini black holes that were created at the Big Bang are believed to pass through Earth every day. They are speculated to have masses in the trillionths of a kilogram.

The nucleus of an atom is one hundred thousand times smaller than the atom itself. That is comparable to the head of a pin in the center of a football stadium.

SHUTTLE SCUTTLE

After 135 missions, the space shuttle was scuttled in 2011.

The combined distance traveled by all the space shuttle missions is 593 million miles.

Some interesting things flew aboard the space shuttle over the years, including a Buzz Lightyear doll, a light-saber prop from the *Star Wars* series, *Star Trek* creator Gene Roddenberry's ashes, dirt from Yankee Stadium, home plate from Shea Stadium, and three NASCAR start flags.

FASTER THAN A SPEEDING BULLET

Today's fastest spaceship would take ten thousand years to reach the nearest star.

Light travels at 1 million times the speed of sound.

HUBBLE HUBBUB

Edwin Hubble, the scientist credited with the discovery that the universe is expanding, and the namesake of the Hubble Space Telescope, has been accused of censoring the work of rival scientist Georges Lemaître, who made the same observation two years earlier.

SHARPER IMAGE

Magnetic resonance imaging (MRI) machines vibrate the hydrogen atoms in the body with a magnet sixty thousand times stronger than Earth's magnetic field. This causes them to emit radio waves that can be used to map the inside of the body.

TRUTH BE TOLD

Psychologist William Moulton Marston invented the systolic blood pressure test, which is used in polygraph tests. He is also the creator of the comic book superhero Wonder Woman, who uses her Lasso of Truth to force anyone it ensnares to tell the truth.

DOES ANYBODY REALLY KNOW WHAT TIME IT IS?

Canadian Sir Sandford Fleming first had the idea of twenty-four world time zones in 1878.

Cesium atomic clocks are accurate to about five parts in one hundred thousand billion when averaged over one day, meaning they are accurate to one second in 1.4 million years.

Cesium is a silvery-gold, soft metal. It is the most alkaline element and is liquid at just above room temperature (82°F).

The National Institute of Standards and Technology in Boulder, Colorado, is home to NIST-F1, the most precise clock in the world, accurate to one second in 3.7 billion years.

GET SMART

The median score for IQ tests is set at 100.

Ninety-five percent of people score between 70 and 130 on IQ tests.

Average IQ scores have been rising at a rate of three points per decade for the last one hundred years.

Higher crime rates are found among those individuals who have IQs between 80 and 90.

College professors, research scientists, and neurosurgeons have an average IQ above 135.

A 2011 study found that high school students who chewed gum during math class got better grades and did better on standardized tests.

HOT STUFF

In 2011, researchers at the Brookhaven Relativistic Heavy Ion Collider on Long Island smashed together two gold atoms at near the speed of light and produced the highest human-made temperature ever—7 trillion degrees Fahrenheit. This temperature is 250,000 times hotter than the center of the sun and approaches that believed to have been generated by the Big Bang.

In 2011, a new particle was discovered in the world of physics—the neutral Xi-sub-b—a heavier version of a neutron. It was created for an instant at the Fermilab Tevatron particle accelerator in Batavia, Illinois.

WHODUNIT

Prior to the use of fingerprints, something known as the Bertillon System was used to identify criminals. It used the distances between different bony body parts, which were reduced to a formula that was assumed would be unique to each person. However, in 1903, twin bothers were misidentified using the system, while fingerprints provided positive identification.

John Dillinger dipped his fingertips in acid to remove his fingerprints. However, he could still be identified by the prints lower down on his fingers.

There are at least eighty different methods to find latent fingerprints on an object.

The latent fingerprints of prepubescent children only last a few hours since they lack the waxy oils of adults.

The first use of ballistic fingerprinting—using the marks made on a bullet to identify the gun that fired it—to convict someone in a court of law occurred in 1902.

PAPER OR PLASTIC?

A 2011 study by the Environmental Agency of Britain found that thin plastic shopping bags have a lower carbon footprint than reusable plastic, cloth, or paper bags. A cloth bag would need to be used 131 times to equal the low carbon footprint of thin plastic bags.

Cloth bags have been found to be breeding grounds for harmful bacteria and washing them frequently increases their carbon footprint.

THE BOOB TUBE

American Philo Farnsworth designed the first television at the age of fourteen.

In 1927, Secretary of Commerce Herbert Hoover and his wife became the first people to be broadcast live on television between two cities. They stood in a Washington, DC, funeral home and were beamed to an AT&T laboratory in Manhattan. Mrs. Hoover worried that TV might be used to read viewers' minds.

The first two commercial radio networks in the United States were NBC Red and NBC Blue. The Federal Communications Commission forced NBC to divest itself of NBC Blue in 1942. It became ABC in 1944.

Originally, there were only two hours of television broadcasting a week, in New York City. At the time, only about two hundred TVs had been sold. Most were in bars or department store windows.

PHONY FACTS

As of 2010, some rotary (dial) phones were still in service. Telephone exchanges can still handle their calls.

Early telephones had a crank on them that turned a magnet to produce an electric current that ran down the line and rang a bell on the phone at the other end.

Ships use sound-powered phones that can operate without power in emergency situations. These phones convert the sound power from a person's voice into an electric current that transmits the sound to the phone at the other end.

Martin Cooper of Motorola made the first cell phone call in New York City, on Sixth Avenue near the Hilton Hotel, in 1973, on a brick-size phone that weighed thirty ounces.

Ten years later, Motorola introduced the sixteen-ounce DynaTAC phone, which cost $3,500 a pop.

The longest-distance phone call in history was made in 1969 when President Richard Nixon phoned astronauts Neil Armstrong and Buzz Aldrin on the moon.

FALL GUYS

William Rankin survived the highest fall through a cumulonimbus thunderhead cloud when he bailed out of his USMC F-8 jet over forty-seven thousand feet above South Carolina in 1959 with no pressure suit. The −50°C temperatures caused him to suffer frostbite almost immediately, and the lack of air pressure caused him to bleed from his ears, nose, and eyes. It was five minutes before his parachute deployed, and when it did, strong updrafts kept him aloft in the storm for forty minutes. He had to keep his mouth closed for much of the time to avoid drowning from the intense rain all around him.

USAF pilot Joseph Kittinger holds the world record for highest skydive. In 1960 he jumped out of a plane at 102,800 feet and fell for 84,800 feet, reaching a speed of 614 miles per hour, before opening his parachute.

The highest altitude and fastest speed a pilot ever ejected from was eighty thousand feet at Mach 3.825.

BIG BIRD

The Lockheed C-5 Galaxy is a huge military transport plane that has a wingspan of 222 feet and a length of 247 feet, which is longer than the first manned flight of the Wright brothers.

POOP BURGERS

A researcher in Tokyo has come up with a novel way of disposing of the country's sewage waste—he has developed a process to make it edible. By reacting sewage with soya and coloring it red, he has created a meat substitute that tastes like beef and contains 63 percent protein, 25 percent carbohydrates, 9 percent minerals, and 3 percent lipids. Thankfully, this poop meat still costs ten to twenty times what real beef does.

TROPHY TREES

Each year America's biggest tree representatives from 751 native species are ranked by the conservation group American Forest. In 2011, Florida led the nation with 106 champion trees. Hawaii, North Dakota, and Wyoming had none on the list.

Oaks are the trees most frequently struck by lightning.

THE OUT-OF-TOWNERS

More than 50 percent of the damaging invasive plants found worldwide were introduced by escaping from botanical gardens.

ATTACK OF THE GIANT HOGWEED

Giant hogweed is an introduced invasive plant in America. This weed, which is native to central Asia and can reach heights of twenty-three feet, has invaded New York

State. The sap of this monster can cause phytophoto-dermatitis, or severe skin inflammation, when the skin is exposed to sunlight. Contact with the sap also causes burning blisters that will leave purplish black scars that may last for years. Minute quantities in the eye can cause temporary or permanent blindness.

PLANT PRODUCTS

Linseed oil comes from flaxseed. It is used as a binder in linoleum and as the base for oil paints.

Frankincense and myrrh are dried tree sap.

Ancient trees buried for fifty thousand years in New Zealand peat bogs are being dug up and used to make furniture.

TATER TIME

One-half acre of potatoes produces enough food to feed a family of four for a year.

There are five thousand varieties of potatoes in the Andes.

The potato was domesticated eight thousand years ago.

Most wild potatoes are bitter or poisonous.

The Irish potato famine resulted from the fact that just one variety of potato was grown throughout Ireland, so no plants had any resistance to the blight that killed them all. The planting of several different varieties would have increased the chances that one variety would have had resistance to the disease.

All McDonald's french fries are made from Russet Burbank potatoes.

RED HOTS

The hottest pepper in the world is the Trinidad Butch T, which is three hundred times hotter than the hottest jalapeño.

SCIENCE SHORTS

The leaf blower was invented in the late 1950s as a tool to spread pesticides.

Early man used meteorites as a source of iron.

Flags will stand straight out in winds of thirty miles per hour or higher.

Bell Labs patented the laser in 1960.

One Leland Clark invented an oxygenated perfluoro-carbon fluid in 1966 that allowed a mouse to breathe the liquid while totally submerged in it for several hours.

Water jets containing sand fired at sixty thousand pounds per square inch (psi) of pressure are used to cut thick panes of glass.

Each day some 200 billion spam emails are sent, representing about 90 percent of all email traffic (volume).

No animals over twenty-two pounds survived the meteor that struck Earth 65 million years ago.

BODY WORKS

CURIOUS CONDITIONS

Ice-chewing disorder, known as pagophagia, is more common in women. Some people eat up to two gallons of ice a day. Doctors believe those with iron deficiencies crave ice more than others. It is estimated that about 16 percent of females between the ages of sixteen and nineteen are compulsive ice chewers.

Some people who tan as much as eight to fifteen times a month can become addicted to the endorphins produced by the ultraviolet light they are exposed to. Those who suddenly stop tanning may experience endorphin withdrawal symptoms that can include nausea and dizziness.

There is a medical condition known as "wallet neuropathy," where men who keep overly fat wallets in their back pockets may experience compressed nerves and twisting of the spine, resulting in backaches and numbness.

People who suffer from superior canal dehiscence syndrome may experience a symptom called autophony, where they begin to hear sounds from within the body. In severe cases, individuals may hear their heart beating or even their eyeballs moving. The noise from chewing food can become deafening.

Burning mouth syndrome causes sufferers to experience the intense sensation of scalding water in various parts of the mouth. No reason for this condition has been found.

Twelve million Americans have restless leg syndrome and experience a burning, creeping, tugging sensation in the legs and may feel as if bugs are crawling on them.

Morgellons disease is a condition where sufferers feel as if something is crawling, biting, or stinging their skin, and they may have rashes or sores. No cause for this condition has been found and many researchers believe it is a form of delusional parasitosis, where sufferers think they are infested with parasites.

A skin condition known as "fiddler's neck" is common to violin, viola, and cello players. The repeated pressure of the instrument causes scaling, cysts, and pustules on the left side of the neck below the jaw.

Rose gardeners' disease is caused by the *Sporothrix* fungus, which enters the body after the skin is pricked by a rose thorn or through other cuts while handling vegetation. Skin lesions and boils can result.

"Broken heart syndrome" is a ballooning of the bottom of the heart that can be caused by grief or extreme stress.

Several people who were injured during the tornado that struck Joplin, Missouri, in 2011 came down with a rare, deadly fungal infection known as zygomycosis. Fungi carried on dirt and plant debris that penetrated the skin of the twister's victims caused several infections. This rapidly spreading infection gets into the blood and results in tissue necrosis (death) in areas such as the nasal cavity, mouth, and facial skin.

In 2011, a twenty-two-year-old woman was found to have supernumerary breast tissue, or a nipple, on the sole of her foot.

Also in 2011, an Englishwoman with two uteruses gave birth to twins, one from each uterus.

CREATIVE CURES

In parts of India, people swallow small, live fish to cure asthma.

In China, bee stings are used to treat arthritis, rheumatism, and nasal inflammation.

The drinking of cow's urine is practiced across Asia to cure a host of different ailments.

In Peru, pregnant women let a dolphin touch their belly because they believe the high-frequency sounds the animals make promote neuron growth and help the baby's brain development.

DIRTY DINING

In the ten years from 1999 to 2009, the number of hospital visits in the United States for pica—the eating of dirt and other abnormal substances—nearly doubled.

RED RIBBONS

Between 2007 and 2009, the worldwide number of people infected with HIV, the virus that causes AIDS, leveled off at 33.4 million.

> AIDS was first identified in 1981. Researchers were able to trace the disease back to possible cases in 1969.

HIV has never been found in animals, but other primates carry similar immunodeficiency viruses.

> Red ribbons, which are worn to support AIDS awareness, were first worn by supporters of drug and alcohol abuse prevention after the kidnapping and murder of DEA agent Enrique Camarena while he was working undercover in Mexico in 1988.

A CASE OF THE MONDAYS

In Tokyo, there are 20 percent more heart attacks on Mondays than the other days of the week.

FEAST AND FAMINE

There are 1 billion overweight people in the world and 800 million who are undernourished.

UPON FURTHER REVIEW

Far from aggravating an ulcer, hot peppers actually help *reduce* stomach acid.

New research shows that stretching before distance running actually decreases energy and performance.

BAD MEDICINE

All medications have some side effects. Some, in rare cases, are rather peculiar:

Pepto-Bismol has been known to give some individuals a black tongue that feels furry.

Users of Ambien may engage in sleep eating, driving, and sex, none of which they are able to recall when they wake up.

In rare cases, men who take too much Viagra may experience "blue vision." The rods in their eyes become sensitized and they see everything with a blue tint.

Mirapex, which is prescribed for restless leg syndrome, may produce a compulsion to eat, gamble, and have sex.

The antismoking drug Chantix can produce nightmares.

Vasotec, an old blood pressure medicine, made some patients lose their sense of taste and smell.

The cancer drug Xeloda has the potential to result in hand-foot syndrome. Symptoms include blistering, bleeding skin ulcers, peeling skin, and inflamed palms and soles. Some users actually totally lose their fingerprints.

Statins, such as Lipitor, can cause amnesia.

NOT SO SWEET NEWS

Diabetes, a condition where a person has high blood sugar, is more formally known as diabetes mellitus.

In the United States, 8.3 percent of the population has diabetes.

Approximately 26.9 percent of Americans over the age of sixty-five have diabetes.

Diabetes is the seventh-leading cause of death in America.

Diabetes is the leading cause of new cases of blindness among adults ages twenty to seventy-four.

SOBERING NEWS

Alcohol-related deaths worldwide exceed those from AIDS, tuberculosis, and violence combined.

BLACK AND WHITE

A biracial man and a biracial woman have a one in a million chance of conceiving fraternal twins together, one of which is black and one of which is white.

IT'S ALL IN THE GENES

Most DNA is found in a cell's mitochondria, not the nucleus.

DNA was discovered in 1869, by Swiss biochemist Friedrich Miescher.

Bacteriologist Oswald Avery figured out that DNA was the genetic blueprint in 1943.

A Japanese flowering plant—*Paris japonica*—has the longest known genome, with almost 150 billion base pairs. By comparison, the human genome contains 2.3 billion bases.

About 8 percent of the human genome originated in viruses.

The lowly one-celled paramecium has nearly double the number of genes as does a human cell—almost forty thousand.

CAVEMEN COUSINS

Humans and Neanderthals interbred thousands of years ago. Scientists believe that some modern human immune

system genes were passed down from these inter-matings.

Neanderthals shared 99.7 percent of their genome with humans.

SKINTIGHT GENES

A 2011 study found the long-sought-after genes that make some people naturally skinny. There are twenty-eight genes found on chromosome 16 that cause those without them to be forty-three times more likely to be morbidly obese than people who have them. People who have a double set of these genes are far more likely to be skinny. One in two thousand people have this double set. Men who do are twenty-three times more likely to be underweight and women five times more likely.

HIGH ON HORMONES

Women with high levels of estrogen have higher-pitched voices.

Men with higher levels of testosterone have deeper voices and father more children.

Mothers who have higher than normal levels of cortisol (a steroid hormone released by the adrenal gland while under stress) during late pregnancy may have children with lower IQs.

A greater percentage of men have shorter index fingers than ring fingers than do women. It is believed individuals that were exposed to more testosterone in the womb have shorter index fingers.

FOR CRYING OUT LOUD

Humans are the only species that shed emotional tears.

The smell of a woman's emotional tears has been shown to lower testosterone levels in men, thereby reducing aggression and sexual arousal.

A woman's blood contains 50 to 60 percent more of the hormone prolactin than a man's. This chemical helps women produce milk and also aids in tear production, making them cry more easily.

Women also have narrower tear ducts than men, meaning that tears are more likely to flow out and down the cheeks.

BEAUTY SLEEP

A study by people who specialize in such things recommends that women sleep on their backs if they want to retard facial wrinkling and maintain pert breasts. Sleeping on the side or stomach smushes the face and causes the breasts to dangle and sag.

MICROBIAL MILIEU

There are four pounds of bacteria in the average human gut.

The mouth is home to some one thousand different bacterial species.

Different sides of the same tooth can have totally different microbes.

Scientists at the Belly Button Biodiversity Project have found 662 new species of bacteria dwelling in people's navels out a total of 1,400 species found.

A new species of bacteria has been discovered that can live on an exclusive diet of caffeine.

CONTAGIOUS CALIFORNIA

The plague, or Black Death, entered San Francisco in 1900, carried by fleas on rats aboard a ship from China. The epidemic, which was concealed by public officials, abated in 1908, after 172 deaths. The plague had moved to Oakland by 1919 and finally in 1924 to Los Angeles, where thirty-seven people died.

WARTS AND ALL

There are more than one hundred kinds of viruses that can cause warts.

About 10 percent of children and adolescents have warts at any given time.

About 22 percent of people will have warts during childhood, most commonly between the ages of nine and sixteen.

One percent of sexually active adults get genital warts. Women who smoke or use oral contraceptives are at a greater risk of developing genital warts.

Doctors aren't sure why, but butchers have an abnormally high occurrence (near 50 percent) of warts on their hands and lower arms, probably due to frequent contact with raw meat.

FECAL FINGERS

Coxsackie viruses live in the human digestive tract and are spread from person to person by unwashed hands and surfaces contaminated with feces. Coxsackie viruses are a common cause of disease in children. Symptoms can range from mild flu-like symptoms to hand, foot, and mouth disease, causing painful red blisters in the throat and on the tongue, gums, and others parts of the mouth, as well as the palms of the hands and soles of the feet. These viruses are named for the town of Coxsackie, New York, where researchers collected fecal samples from polio patients in studying that disease and inadvertently discovered Coxsackie viruses.

LYMEYS

Lyme disease is most prevalent in Connecticut, New Jersey, New York, and Pennsylvania.

Famous sufferers from Lyme disease include George W. Bush, Senator Chuck Schumer, singer Daryl Hall, and author Amy Tan.

Aside from Lyme disease, ticks can carry at least eight other major diseases, and individuals can be infected with more than one of them from a single tick bite.

The U.S. blood supply is being threatened by another tick-borne pathogen, a malaria-like parasite known as *Babesia*, which causes a flu-like disease (babesiosis) that can be fatal to premature babies and elderly people who receive tainted transfusions. There currently is no specific test that can be done to check donated blood for this disease. Babesiosis is most prevalent in ticks in eastern Long Island, Nantucket Island, and Martha's Vineyard, but is more widespread in the blood supply.

FEAR NOT

Several of the stranger phobias some people suffer from follow:

Agyrophobia is the fear of streets or crossing streets.

Anglophobia is the fear of England and the English.

Anuptaphobia is the fear of staying single.

Apotemnophobia is the fear of amputees.

Asymmetriphobia is the fear of asymmetrical things.

Bibliophobia is the fear of books.

Cacophobia is the fear of ugliness.

Catoptrophobia is the fear of mirrors.

Chionophobia is the fear of snow.

Clinophobia is the fear of colors.

Decidophobia is the fear of making decisions.

Dextrophobia is the fear of things at the right side of the body.

Dutchphobia is the fear of the Dutch.

Epistemophobia is the fear of knowledge.

Ereuthrophobia is the fear of blushing.

Ergophobia is the fear of work.

Gerontophobia is the fear of old people.

Geumaphobia is the fear of taste.

Graphophobia is the fear of writing or handwriting.

Heliophobia is the fear of the sun.

Hippopotomonstrosesquippedaliophobia is the fear of (gasp!) long words.

Hylophobia is the fear of forests.

Kainolophobia is the fear of anything new.

Linonophobia is the fear of string.

Logophobia is the fear of words.

Macrophobia is the fear of long waits.

Metrophobia is the fear of poetry.

Nomatophobia is the fear of names.

Ombrophobia is the fear of rain.

Panophobia is the fear of everything.

Parthenophobia is the fear of virgins or young girls.

Pentheraphobia is the fear of mothers-in-law.

Petronophobia is the fear of being tickled with feathers.

Philemaphobia is the fear of kissing.

Phobiatriviaphobia is the fear of trivia about phobias.

Placophobia is the fear of tombstones.

Proctophobia is the fear of rectums.

Pupaphobia is the fear of puppets.

Sinistrophobia is the fear of things to the left or left-handed people.

Symmetrophobia is the fear of symmetry.

Urophobia is the fear of urinating.

@#$%&*!

A 2011 British study found that swearing increases one's tolerance for pain, especially if the person doing so doesn't usually curse that much.

BURN, BABY, BURN

In a 2011 study, men who biked intensely on a stationary bike for forty-five minutes burned an average of 519 calories and, as a bonus, continued to burn an extra 190 calories over the next fourteen hours, compared to days that they had not worked out. This indicates that any intense workout will continue to burn many extra calories after the exercising has ended.

DIRTY DOCTORS

Another 2011 study found that 63 percent of doctors' uniforms carried potential pathogens. Fourteen percent of nurses' uniforms carried antibiotic-resistant bacteria.

SUGAR POP

The average American male consumes 175 calories a day from sugar-sweetened drinks. The average female consumes 95 calories a day from such drinks. The American Heart Association recommends no more than 450 calories a week from sugar-sweetened soft drinks.

YOUR TAX DOLLARS AT WORK

In 2009, the National Institutes of Health did a study titled "The Association Between Penis Size and Sexual Health Among Men Who Have Sex with Men." The study determined the preferred sexual positions of men according to their size.

IN TOUCH

Human fingertips are capable of feeling grooves in a surface that are just two-millionths of an inch deep.

Human skin can detect temperature differences of just 0.01°F.

HOLY MOLEY

Researchers at Kings College in London have found that people with more than one hundred moles will probably get fewer wrinkles and live longer. The downside is that "moley" people have an increased chance of getting cancer.

Ten percent of white people are considered moley.

UNDER THE KNIFE

One Cindy Jackson of Great Britain holds the record for most elective cosmetic surgery procedures performed in a lifetime—fifty-two. She has spent more than $100,000 thus far trying to "improve" her looks.

BODY BRIEFS

The tongue is made of sixteen muscles.

One-half of the human body's weight is oxygen.

The top source of food poisoning in the United States is poultry.

Keraunomedicine is the study of lightning injuries and their treatment.

There are 7,000 trillion trillion atoms in the average human body.

Feathers, Fins, and Fur

FROM THE TOP DOWN

The increase or decrease in animals at the top of the food chain can affect an ecosystem in many ways. A few recent examples follow:

As the lion population in Africa has decreased, the baboon population has boomed.

When wolves were reintroduced into Yellowstone National Park, the elk and deer populations decreased, thus allowing creek-side willow trees to flourish and provide needed habitat for several other species, including beavers, which were nearly extinct in the park.

Some whales dive to the ocean bottom to feed and then deposit deep-sea nutrients in surface waters through their feces. This helps plankton and other upper-water species to thrive. When whale populations crash, so does other life in the upper ecosystem.

When wildebeest numbers plummeted from a disease in parts of Africa, the woody plants they grazed on proliferated to such an extent that wildfires became commonplace. After a vaccine was used to eradicate the disease, the natural grasslands returned and wildfires became less frequent.

Sea lion numbers began to drop in the late 1980s due to the overfishing of their main food source. Sea lions are the favored prey of killer whales, and the sea lion decline led to the killer whales eating sea otters, reducing their numbers in Alaska by 90 percent.

LONG-DISTANCE VOYAGERS

In 1988, a horde of locusts flew from North Africa to the Caribbean.

CAT SCRATCH FEVER

Cat scratch disease is caused by exposure to cat saliva or being bitten or scratched by a feline. Bacteria in the cat's saliva leads to swelling of the lymph nodes.

Each year, there are twenty-two thousand diagnosed cases of the disease in the United States.

It is believed that all cats are infected with the bacteria at some point in their lives.

CALICO CORNER

Almost all calico cats are female. The one in three thousand that is male has an extra X chromosome and is thus sterile.

WORLDWIDE WEBS

Tarantulas can shoot silk from their feet to allow them to walk on vertical surfaces without falling.

> There is a kind of algae that lives in the Atacama Desert, the driest place on Earth, which grows on spiderwebs that catch the morning dew, giving the algae the water it needs to survive.

Diving bell spiders take air bubbles with them when they go underwater. They can get enough air from one bubble to survive twenty-four hours without surfacing.

> The Australian funnel-web spider has fangs so powerful that it can bite right through a hiking boot. The spider's venom can kill a person in under an hour.

The male funnel-web spider chemically puts the female into a stupor before mating with her, so she will not devour him.

> The male nursery web spider brings the female a silk-wrapped insect to feast on to keep her occupied while he copulates with her.

The bite of the Brazilian wandering spider can cause a man to have a painful erection lasting many hours. Researchers are investigating the venom for treating erectile dysfunction.

Himalayan jumping spiders live in the Himalayas at twenty-two thousand feet. This is the highest altitude known for any terrestrial animal. They subsist on stray insects that are blown up the mountainside by wind.

Some jumping spiders are vegetarians.

MY DOG'S BETTER THAN YOUR DOG

In 2011, there were six new breeds at the Westminster Kennel Club Annual Dog Show—the Boykin Spaniel, the Bluetick Coonhound, the Redbone Coonhound, the Cane Corso, the Leonberger, and the Icelandic Sheepdog.

As of 2010, the terrier group has won 45 out of the 103 Best in Show prizes awarded since 1907.

The Wire Fox Terrier has won the most Best in Show awards—thirteen.

One particular Wire Fox Terrier won Best in Show three times from 1907 to 1909.

The Golden Retriever and Labrador Retriever breeds have never won Best in Show.

The oldest Best in Show winner was a ten-year-old Sussex Spaniel in 2009. The youngest winner was a nine-month-old Rough Collie in 1929.

DOG DAYS

The average dog can learn to understand 165 words.

The pit bull breed is the result of a cross between a bulldog and a terrier.

A trained dog can detect colon cancer, by smelling a stool sample, with as much accuracy as a colonoscopy.

The Boston terrier was the first American breed of dog.

Pharaoh hounds blush when excited, causing their face, nose, and the insides of their ears to turn a rosy pink.

The borzoi used to be called the Russian wolfhound.

Because of the slim hips of the female French bulldog, the males are unable to mount her. Breeders typically artificially inseminate this breed.

Most French bulldog puppies are delivered by Cesarean section.

Short-nosed dogs have short tongues that are inefficient at dissipating heat through evaporation, and thus the dogs have a hard time tolerating high temperatures.

MUNCH OF THE PENGUINS

The cost to clean each penguin affected by the *Exxon Valdez* oil spill in 1989 was $80,000. Two of the little guys were promptly eaten by a killer whale minutes after their release back into the wild.

DEER ME

Instead of antlers, male Siberian musk deer have long fangs that they use to fight other males.

> The scent gland of the male Siberian musk deer is the source of musk, the most expensive animal product in the world, selling for as much as $45,000 per kilogram.

Other animals, including the muskrat, musk duck, musk turtle, musk ox, musk shrew, and musk beetle have musk glands, as well as some snakes, alligators, and crocodiles.

> The word "musk" comes from the Sanskrit word for "testicle."

CRYPTOZOOLOGY

In 2007, a Bigfoot was purportedly photographed in Pennsylvania's Allegheny Forest.

> The word "Sasquatch" comes from the Salish Native American word *Sésquac*, meaning "hairy man."

TAZ

The Tasmanian devil has the strongest bite of any animal relative to its size.

Tasmanian devil mothers give birth to twenty to thirty young, all of whom must crawl from the vagina to the pouch and fight for one of her four teats. The lucky four will latch on for one hundred days. The unfortunate others will be eaten by Mom.

The Tasmanian devil is expected to become extinct in the next ten to forty years because of a fatal, transmissible cancer that is rapidly spreading throughout their population.

EASY DOES IT

Sloths can reach a top speed of five feet per minute when on the ground.

It takes a sloth about a month to digest a meal.

In moist conditions, sloths' fur contains cyanobacteria (blue-green algae) that give it a greenish tint for camouflage. The sloths can lick the algae to obtain nutrients.

GO FISH

The world's biggest freshwater fish is the Mekong catfish. One was caught in Thailand in 2006 that measured nine feet and weighed 646 pounds.

The largest freshwater fish in the United States is the alligator gar. A 327-pound specimen was caught in the Mississippi River in 2011.

MEAT AND EAT

Each year, 1.7 million camels, 24 million water buffaloes, 293 million cows, 518 million sheep, 633 million turkeys, 1.1 billion rabbits, 1.3 billion pigs, 2.6 billion ducks, and 52 billion chickens are killed by humans for food.

BYE-BYE BIRDIE

Each year more than 100 million birds crash into windows in North America. Most of them smash into homes.

About 90,000 birds hit windows in New York City annually.

In 2011, San Francisco passed an ordinance requiring new buildings in parts of the city to use "bird-safe" windows—glass with partially opaque material inside to make it more visible to birds.

Bar-headed geese are the highest-flying birds. They actually fly over the Himalayas during their migrations and reach heights of well over thirty-three thousand feet.

Avocados are toxic to many species of birds.

Male songbirds that sing in a lower, more baritone voice are the most likely to attract a mate. However, birds in urban areas must sing in a higher voice to be heard over the din of city life.

MÉNAGE À SEPT

Tetrahymena thermophilia, a single-celled organism found in pond scum, has seven different sexes, as opposed to two. A member of one sex can mate with any of the other six, meaning that there are twenty-one different possible viable couplings.

LONG IN THE TOOTH

Geoduck clams in Puget Sound can live to be 160 years old.

A tuatara, a kind of reptile found in New Zealand that resembles a lizard, may live for one hundred to two hundred years.

The tube worms that live near deep ocean thermal vents are known to reach the age of 160 years and are believed to be capable of achieving 250 years.

The red sea urchins that are found along the coastline of the Pacific Northwest live to the ripe old age of two hundred years or more.

WORMS FROM HELL

Scientists have recently found small worms that live 0.8 mile beneath the earth's surface, making them the multicellular organism that dwells the deepest underground.

The worm's scientific name—*Helicephalobus mephisto*—is taken from Faust's Mephistopheles.

The worms live by ingesting bacteria.

IN SYNC

Beginning in 2001, blue whales around the world, in various populations, all began singing their songs in deeper tones. Each year since, the songs have continued to get even deeper.

YOUR FLIGHT MAY BE DELAYED

During egg-laying season, diamondback terrapins emerge from the waters that surround JFK Airport in New York and crawl across the runways to adjacent sandy areas to deposit their eggs. Airport personnel have to remove the little guys, and short delays of flights result.

MOTHER FROGGER

Tropical poison dart frog mothers carry their tadpoles, attached to a mucus layer on their backs, to pools of water that collect in bromeliad plants high up in the jungle canopy. The mothers return every few days to deposit a sterile egg in the pool to feed their offspring.

BEE GONE

In the past five years, 45 billion worker honeybees per year have died or disappeared from colony collapse disorder. No one knows what is causing this.

Tropical stingless bees collect the resin from certain trees that contain an antibiotic and carry it back to their hive, where it helps to protect their young from infections.

FLUTTER BUGS

There are about ten times more species of moths than butterflies—between 150,000 and 200,000.

GO *FIGURE*

For each species of fig, there is only one species of wasp that can pollinate it.

ALL ABOUT ANTS

Honeypot ant colonies have members whose only function is to engorge their abdomens with nutritious fluid, serving as a living larder for the colony. They can swell to the size of a grape when fully engorged.

Some ants "farm" scale insects—cottony, stationary bugs that feed on plant sap. The ants will protect the scales from predators and stroke them with their antennae to induce the scales to exude a honeydew liquid. When the ants move to a new colony, they often pack up the scale bugs and bring them along, placing them on a suitable plant nearby.

When the queen of an ant colony dies, the colony can only survive for a few months. Queens are rarely replaced.

Ant colonies often go to war. The victorious colony will carry off the eggs of the vanquished and raise the new ants to be "slave" workers.

The life expectancy of an ant is about forty-five to sixty days.

Worker ants will carry the colony's eggs and larvae deep into the nest at nighttime to protect them from the cold and bring them back near the surface during the day to warm them.

There are about 1 million ants for each person on Earth.

THEY ONLY COME OUT AT NIGHT

Mosquitoes are very prone to drying out. They spend hot, sunny days in shady, humid areas.

Mosquitoes can only fly at about one and a half miles per hour. This is why they are not usually a problem on breezy days or under ceiling fans.

Mosquitoes are most active on nights with a full moon, since this allows them to see better.

Mosquitoes seem to favor people with type O blood.

Vampire bats have infrared heat sensors in their noses that can detect where the highest concentration of blood close to the surface of their prey's skin is to allow them to feed more efficiently.

The animal with the shortest scientific name is the great evening bat—*Ia io*.

PET PROJECT

Eleven percent of Americans have pet fish, while 8 percent own a bird.

Twenty-five percent of Americans have tasted their pet's food.

SLEEPY STORY

Horses only sleep three hours a day, while little brown bats sleep twenty. Giraffes sleep about four and a half hours a day, dogs ten hours a day, cats twelve and a half, and chipmunks fifteen.

A LITTLE FISHY

Sardines are not a specific species of fish, but can be any of several small species of fish related to herring that are pickled and canned.

The word "sardine" comes from the island of Sardinia, where these types of fish flourished.

BABY TALK

A baby eel is known as an elver and a baby jellyfish is an ephyra.

ALIEN INVASION

Rose-ringed parakeets, which are native to India, were somehow introduced to England decades ago. In 1995, there were fifteen hundred of them. By 2011, their numbers had increased to thirty-two thousand.

STAT SHEET

IT'S POTTY TIME

According to studies, the average person spends about three years of their lives sitting on a toilet.

The average person uses 8.6 sheets of toilet paper per trip to the bathroom and a total of fifty-seven sheets a day.

The Pentagon goes through roughly 666 rolls of toilet paper a day.

SUCH A WASTE

Americans throw away about 2.5 million plastic bottles every hour.

BUSINESS BRIEFS

In 2010, General Electric made a $5 billion profit in their U.S. businesses, but paid zero dollars in federal taxes.

In 2011, Apple Computer had more operating cash on hand than the U.S. Treasury—$76.2 billion versus $73.8 billion. Apple also became the most valuable company in the world, surpassing ExxonMobil, with a market capitalization of $343 billion.

Eighty-nine percent of Whole Foods stores are in counties that Barack Obama won in the 2008 election.

Only 16 percent of all board seats at Fortune 500 companies are held by women.

From 2009 to 2011, 14 million Toyota vehicles were recalled because of safety issues.

There are 1.2 million patents pending in the United States. The average waiting period for approval is three years.

Shoplifting costs U.S. retailers $11 billion each year, and American families $450 on household items because stores raise prices to cover the costs of their losses.

Seventy-two percent of grocery store shopping carts have traces of fecal matter on their handles.

About half of people say they keep a toothbrush and toothpaste at work.

BIGGEST LOSERS

In 2010, many American companies lost billions of dollars. The top seven losers:

Freddie Mac lost $14 billion

Fannie Mae lost $14 billion

Sprint Nextel lost $3.5 billion

Energy Future Holdings (an electric utility) lost $2.8 billion

Bank of America lost $2.2 billion

AbitibiBowater (a newsprint maker) lost $1.9 billion

MGM Resorts International lost $1.4 billion

ITSY-BITSY

The average American woman owns four bathing suits.

Americans spent $4.3 billion on swimwear in 2009.

DRIVER DATA

A 2011 study found that drivers who go to court to fight a speeding ticket are 25 percent more likely to be in an accident within the next three years.

One-quarter of those who went to court to fight a speeding summons were found not guilty, had their case dismissed, or were not prosecuted.

Kids are 33 percent safer while being driven in a car by their grandparents than they are in a car driven by their parents.

In a survey, 72 percent of men and 35 percent of women claimed that they were very confident they could change a flat tire.

Drivers of 2005 through 2008 SUV models are 50 percent less likely to die in a crash than are drivers of other cars.

Washington, DC, has an accident rate double the national average. Drivers there can expect to have one accident every 4.8 years on average.

The area of the country with the highest speed limits is West Texas, where some highways allow drivers to go up to eighty-five miles per hour.

SLIPPERY WHEN WET

Weather is a factor in 24 percent of car crashes.

The odds of having a car accident are 70 percent higher in the rain.

HOT WHEELS

The temperature of a closed car can rise nineteen degrees in just ten minutes and forty-three degrees in an hour.

In 2010, forty-nine American children died from being left unattended in hot cars.

DEADLY DATA

An average of forty people die each year on America's ski slopes.

Pilot error is the cause of 38 percent of major air crashes.

On average, 155 people die accidentally each year in America's national parks. Drowning is the number one cause of death in the parks.

On average, one person every two weeks jumps off the 220-foot-tall Golden Gate Bridge. Ninety-eight percent of the jumpers die. Fifteen hundred people have perished since the bridge's opening in 1937.

Prescription painkillers kill two people every hour in the United States and send about forty to the emergency room from overdoses.

Nineteen percent of childhood deaths from choking on food are caused by hot dogs.

Ten thousand American children are taken to emergency rooms each year for injuries caused by cribs.

Each year, 6 million items are delivered in New York City by bike messengers. About twenty-two messengers a year die on the busy streets while doing so.

People who spend six hours a day watching television live about five years less than those who don't watch any TV.

In 2009, there were more drug-related deaths— 37,485—in the United States than traffic deaths. That's about one drug-related death every fourteen minutes.

According to the National Safety Council, the odds of an American dying from various causes are as follows:

Heart disease: 1 in 6

Cancer: 1 in 7

Motor vehicle accident: 1 in 28

Suicide/self-harm: 1 in 112

Accidental poisoning: 1 in 130

Falling: 1 in 171

Firearm assault: 1 in 306

Pedestrian accident: 1 in 649

Motorcycle accident: 1 in 770

Drowning: 1 in 1,123

Fire: 1 in 1,177

Bicycle accident: 1 in 4,717

Firearm accident: 1 in 6,309

Electrocution: 1 in 9,943

Heat exposure: 1 in 12,517

Cataclysmic storm: 1 in 46,044

Insect sting: 1 in 71,623

Legal execution: 1 in 96,691

Dog attack: 1 in 120,864

Earthquake: 1 in 148,756

Flood: 1 in 175,803

Fireworks: 1 in 386,766

Shark attack: 1 in 3,943,110

DOCTOR'S CHOICE

In a 2011 survey only 14 percent of American obstetricians reported having ever performed an abortion.

Of the doctors who did not perform abortions, 52 percent cited their religion as being very important to them. Protestant and Catholic doctors were found less likely to perform the procedure than were Jewish or nonreligious doctors.

Eighty-eight percent of OB-GYNs who did perform abortions were from urban centers.

COOLING ON WARMING

A poll taken in 2001 found that 75 percent of adult Americans believed in the science of global warming. A similar 2011 poll found that just 44 percent did so.

EAT YOUR VEGGIES

According to a 2011 *Consumer Reports* survey, parsnips are the vegetable that people are least likely to eat, followed closely by Swiss chard, bok choy, turnips/rutabagas, and artichokes and eggplant.

DANGEROUS WATERS

In 2010, Somali pirates hijacked fifty-three ships and took 1,181 people hostage.

Worldwide, there were 455 ships taken by pirates in 2010.

Each year about ten thousand shipping containers fall from ships and sink to the bottom of the ocean.

THE UGLY TRUTH

Numerous studies conducted from 1971 to 2009 found, to no one's surprise, that beautiful people are happier than less attractive folks. Better-looking people also earn more money and marry other good-looking people, who also earn more money.

STICK 'EM UP!

In 2010, there were 5,546 bank robberies in the United States, with slightly more than $43 million stolen.

The South led the way with 1,790 bank robberies, followed by the West with 1,691.

COMING OF AGE

About 15 percent of American girls begin puberty at age seven. Ten percent of white girls and 23 percent of black girls start developing breasts by that age.

Girls on average were beginning to grow breasts a year earlier in 2006 than they did in 1991.

WATERWORKS

The greatest users of household water are toilets, accounting for 25.5 percent of usage, followed by washing machines at 22.2 percent and showers at 17.4 percent.

HEALTH REPORT

Forty-seven percent of people worldwide suffer from headache disorders.

Migraine headaches affect one in six women and one in twelve men.

People who are overweight in middle age have an 80 percent higher risk of dementia later in life.

Four in ten men and one in eleven women worldwide are smokers.

Nearly 11 percent of Americans reported smoking marijuana in 2008.

RISQUÉ BUSINESS

Twenty-five percent of toll-free 800 phone numbers have been bought by PrimeTel, a communications company that has assigned most of these 1.7 million numbers to a telephone porn provider.

Each year in the United States, there are 19 million reported cases of sexually transmitted diseases.

Only one-third of sexually active singles use condoms.

THAT BITES

The average claim paid out by the State Farm Insurance Company for dog bites in 2010 was about $25,000. In total, the company paid out $90 million for dog bites in 2010.

COUNTING CALORIES

A 2011 survey of posted calorie counts at chain restaurants found that only 7 percent of the items tested came within ten calories of what they were supposed to be. Nineteen percent were more than one hundred calories higher than posted.

WEDDING BELL BLUES

According to a survey by Real Wedding, it costs the average woman $1,695 to be a bridesmaid, if one figures in the cost of the dress, accessories, gifts, and travel to the wedding, shower, and bachelorette party.

In 2010, 45 percent of American weddings were paid for by the bride's family, 42 percent by the bride and groom, and 12 percent by the groom's family.

Three out of four women surveyed in 2011 said they would not marry an unemployed man.

Ninety-one percent of women say that they would marry for love over money.

Sixty-two percent of women report spending just three hours or less of their waking hours a day with their mate during the workweek.

BEWARE THE BATHROOM

About 234,000 people a year are treated in U.S. emergency rooms for injuries sustained in the bathroom.

Women are more likely to be injured in the bathroom than men.

Two-thirds of bathroom injuries occur in the tub/shower.

CASHING IN

Princeton University is the college from which graduates end up earning the most money later in life. Princeton alumni made an average midcareer salary of $130,000. California Institute of Technology, Harvey Mudd College (in California), Harvard University, and Massachusetts Institute of Technology rounded out the top five.

IT'S THE THOUGHT THAT COUNTS

According to a 2011 survey, the top three gift items that dads say they have enough of to last the rest of their lives are ties, tools, and cologne.

GENDER GAP

Seven in one hundred boys and three in one hundred girls wet their beds at least one time a month.

Women are more likely to be offended and more likely to apologize than men.

Women are more likely than men to give to charities.

Forty-five percent of women have a will, while only 37 percent of men do.

COME FLY WITH ME

By 2012, U.S. airlines were flying 1 billion passengers a year.

The general aviation industry in the United States employs 1.2 million people.

ARMED AND DANGEROUS

More than 1 million people are injured by guns each year.

There are two hundred thousand gun murders every year.

Fifty thousand people use a gun to kill themselves each year.

FOREIGN AFFAIRS

YAKKING IT UP

Tibet's elevation averages sixteen thousand feet.

The snow of Tibet's Mount Kailash is the source of three of Asia's biggest rivers—the Ganges, the Indus, and the Brahmaputra.

Mount Kailish, at 21,638 feet, is the most significant peak in the world that has yet to be scaled. Because the Buddhists and Hindus consider it sacred, the mountain is off-limits to climbers.

In Tibetan, the word *yag* (or *yak*) is used only for the male of the species. The female is called a *nak*.

Dried yak dung is the only natural fuel available on the high, treeless Tibetan plateau.

AMAZON RIVER

During the wet season, the Amazon River can be as much as thirty miles wide.

Twenty percent of the freshwater that enters the world's oceans comes from the Amazon.

There is an underground river four kilometers below the Amazon that follows its course and is one hundred to two hundred kilometers wide.

There are no bridges across the Amazon.

HIGH ON JESUS

The Christ the Redeemer statue, which overlooks Rio de Janiero, is made of reinforced concrete covered with soap-stone.

The statue, which stands 130 feet tall, including the pedestal, took nine years to build and was completed in 1931.

The largest statue of Jesus is 167 feet tall and is found in Swiebodzin, Poland.

RUNNING OUT OF ELBOW ROOM

China is the most populous country, followed by India, the United States, Indonesia, and Brazil.

The world population is expected to increase by 150,000 people a day for the next forty years.

MALE *PURSE*SUIT

In China, men carry purses as a status symbol. Men make up 45 percent of the Chinese luxury handbag market. The highest denomination paper currency note in China is only worth about fifteen dollars. Since China is pretty much still a cash economy, affluent men need to carry large wads of money—too much to fit in a wallet.

DAM IT

There are about forty-eight thousand dams over fifty feet high in the world, half of which are in China.

MOTHER LODES

Russia, Botswana, Australia, the Democratic Republic of the Congo, and South Africa are the world's top five diamond-producing nations, in that order.

South Africa, Australia, the United States, China, and Peru are the top five gold-producing countries.

Peru, Mexico, China, Australia, and Chile are the top five silver producers.

Canada, Australia, Kazakhstan, Russia, and Niger are the top five uranium producers.

LOW OVERHEAD COUNTRIES

Andorra, Costa Rica, Dominica, Grenada, Haiti, Iceland, Kiribati, Liechtenstein, Marshall Islands, Mauritius,

Micronesia, Monaco, Nauru, Palau, Panama, St. Kitts and Nevis, St. Lucia, St. Vincent and the Grenadines, Samoa, San Marino, Solomon Islands, Tuvalu, Vanuatu, and the Vatican have no armies.

Andorra and Tuvalu don't have a national broadcasting system.

Forty-six countries have just one television channel, controlled by the government.

MIND YOUR MANNERS

The standards for good manners vary around the world. For instance:

It is not considered rude in Thailand to pick one's nose in polite company.

Splitting a restaurant bill in France is frowned upon.

In Mexico, it's good form to say *"provecho,"* which means "enjoy," if you catch the eye of someone who is eating, even a stranger.

When out drinking with friends in Australia, it is expected that each person buy the entire group at least one round.

When drinking vodka in Russia, it is a no-no to place the empty bottle on the table. It goes on the floor. And vodka is never mixed, but taken straight.

THE VOTES ARE IN

The legal voting age is sixteen in Austria, Brazil, Cuba, and Nicaragua.

AUTO ZONE

Monaco has the most vehicles per capita—863 for every one thousand residents. The United States is number two at 809, followed by Iceland at 767, Luxembourg at 747, and New Zealand at 733.

> The Central African Republic is the nation with the lowest number of vehicles per one thousand people— 0.3—followed by Bangladesh, Togo, São Tomé, Ethiopia, and Liberia.

GOOD-BYE, GIRLS

The practice of sex selection—using ultrasound and abortion to ensure the birth of a boy—has lowered the number of baby girls that would have been born in Asia by about 160 million. That's more than the entire female population of the United States.

> In China, the ratio of boys born to girls is 121 to 100. In India it's 112 to 100. Sex selection is also prevalent in Armenia, the Balkans, and Georgia.

By 2013, one in ten men in China will not have a female counterpart to marry and have children with and may spend their lives alone. This situation is known as *fenquing*, or "angry youth."

FAMILY PLANNING

The age of marriage with parental consent in Uruguay is twelve for girls and fourteen for boys. In France, it's fourteen for girls and sixteen for boys.

The average age of first-time mothers in Spain is thirty. In Nigeria, it's twenty.

Abortion is illegal for any reason in Chile, El Salvador, the Holy See, Iraq, Laos, Maldives, Malta, Nicaragua, and Niger.

LOST YOUR MARBLES

The Greek Parthenon, in Athens, once served as a mosque and had a minaret.

The Parthenon is said to be the most copied building in history.

There are seventy thousand different pieces of marble making up the Parthenon, each one unique in size and shape.

The Parthenon was used as an ammunition dump by the Ottoman Turks in 1687. A Venetian bombardment caused the ammo inside to explode, severely damaging the structure.

In the early 1800s, Englishman Thomas Bruce, Seventh Earl of Elgin, received permission from the Ottoman authorities to remove about half of the surviving marble sculptures from the Parthenon and ship them back to England. Known as the Elgin Marbles, they are still there today, on display at the British Museum, much to the consternation of the Greek government, who would like them returned to the newly renovated Parthenon.

ROYAL RULES

Only Protestants can ascend to the throne in England. Catholics and those married to Catholics are banned forever from doing so.

Only Lutherans can take the throne in Denmark, Norway, and Sweden.

In Belgium and Spain, one must be Catholic to become king or queen.

In the Netherlands, only Protestants through the House of Orange are eligible to ascend to the throne.

GREASED PALMS

One in four people in the world paid a bribe in 2010. One in two people in India did so.

Singapore has been rated the least corrupt nation in the world by Transparency International.

PRAISE THE LORD

There are an estimated twenty thousand different Protestant religious denominations worldwide.

SLACKER NATIONS

Many countries guarantee workers at companies a specific number of paid days off. For example, employees who work a five-day week and have been with a company for ten years in Brazil and Lithuania are guaranteed forty-one paid days off a year. Following close behind are Finland, France, and Russia with forty days off, and Austria and Malta with thirty-eight days off.

The United States has no law guaranteeing any paid days off. China is the only country where the average worker gets fewer paid days off than America.

WORLD TOUR

Afghanistan has been inhabited for fifty thousand years.

Afghanistan's currency is the afghani.

Albania's currency is the lek.

Algeria is the biggest Arab country and the largest nation in Africa.

The Principality of Andorra's capital city—Andorra la Vella—is the capital city in Europe at the highest elevation. Catalan is the official language.

Andorra has two coprinces. One is the president of the French Republic. The other is the bishop of Urgell, Catalonia, Spain, who is appointed by the Vatican.

The currency of Angola is the kwanza. The capital is Luanda.

Argentina is the largest Spanish-speaking country in the world and the eighth largest by size.

Argentina still claims sovereignty over the Falkland Islands and South Georgia and the South Sandwich Islands, although the United Kingdom exercises authority over them.

Armenia is not recognized by Pakistan.

The Kingdom of Armenia was the first state to adopt Christianity as its religion, in the early fourth century.

Armenia's currency is the dram.

Australia was discovered by Dutch explorers in 1606.

The name "Australia" derives from the Latin *australis*, meaning "southern."

Passports issued in Australia now have a third sex category—"X"—for intersex people who are not fully male or female.

Languages spoken in Austria include German, Croatian, Hungarian, and Slovene.

Azerbaijan was the first democratic secular republic in the Muslim world. Its currency is the manat.

"Bahrain" means "two seas" in Arabic. The Al Khalifa family has ruled Bahrain since 1783.

The currency of Bangladesh is the taka.

Belarus lost one-third of its population during World War II.

Belgium seceded from the Netherlands in 1830.

Belgium, Luxembourg, and the Netherlands are considered the Low Countries.

Belize is the only Central American country where English is the official language.

Bermuda has more churches per capita than any other country in the world.

Bhutan was ranked by *Business* magazine in 2006 as the happiest country in Asia and the eighth happiest in the world. Its currency is the ngultrum, which is subdivided into one hundred chetrums.

Bolivia is officially known as the Plurinational State of Bolivia to recognize the country's multiethnic makeup and indigenous peoples.

Bolivia has had 192 coups since its independence in 1825, the most of any nation.

Bosnia and Herzegovina has a three-member presidency made up of one member from each major ethnic group, although the central government is weak and the country is highly decentralized.

The currency of Botswana is the pula.

Brazil is the largest Portuguese-speaking country in the world. Its currency is the real.

At the end of 2007, there were officially 150,000 unsolved murders in Brazil.

The most expensive birthday party ever thrown was the fiftieth birthday of the Sultan of Brunei, which cost a whopping $27.2 million in 1996.

The currency of Bulgaria is the lev, which means "lion." One lev equals one hundred stotinki.

Burkina Faso means "land of upright people." Its capital is Ouagadougou.

Burma's (Myanmar's) currency is the kyat.

Burma, Liberia, and the United States are the only countries in the world that do not totally use the metric system.

Burundi is a small central African country. Its capital is Bujumbura.

The world's biggest religious building is the Hindu temple Angkor Wat in Cambodia.

There are more than two hundred linguistic groups in Cameroon.

A DUI offense is a felony in Canada, even if it occurs in the United States, and, as such, can be used to deny Americans entry into that country.

Cape Verde is comprised of ten islands off the coast of Western Africa.

More than 40 percent of the legal cases brought to court in the Central African Republic involve sorcery or witchcraft.

Only 9 percent of the people in Chad and Niger have access to toilets with septic or sewerage connections.

Chile's Cape Horn—the southernmost point in the Americas—*is* shaped like a horn, but it was actually named by Dutch navigator Willem Schouten, in 1616, for his hometown—Hoorn.

One person every five seconds in China is killed in an automobile accident.

China imports chopsticks from the United States.

In Beijing officials hold a monthly car registration lottery. The only way citizens get a registration for a new car is through the lottery, where the odds of winning are only thirty-five to one.

China recognizes fifty-six ethnic minorities.

Colombia shares a maritime border with Jamaica, Haiti, and the Dominican Republic.

Comoros had twenty coups, or coup attempts, between 1975 and 2005.

The Democratic Republic of the Congo (formerly Zaire) is the most populous French-speaking country in the world.

While the Democratic Republic of the Congo is the second-poorest country in the world based on its GDP per capita, it is considered the richest country when judged by its untapped raw minerals—estimated value $24 trillion.

The Republic of the Congo, also known as the Congo, lies to the west of the Democratic Republic of the Congo.

Costa Rica plans to become the first carbon-neutral country by 2021.

Hundreds of nearly perfect carved stone spheres have been found in the jungles of Costa Rica. Ranging in size from a few centimeters in diameter to more than six feet, they are believed to be between five hundred and twelve hundred years old.

The capital of Côte d'Ivoire is Yamoussoukro.

The currency of Croatia is the kuna. The word "kuna" means "marten" in Croatian, as marten pelts were used as currency at one time. One hundred lipa equal one kuna.

Cuba used to be a possession of the United States.

The oldest known domestication of cats occurred on Cyprus circa 7500 BC.

The Czech Republic was known as the Lands of the Bohemian Crown until 1918, when it seceded from the Austro-Hungarian Empire and became Czechoslovakia. In 1993, it split into the Czech Republic and Slovakia.

The Kingdom of Denmark is comprised of Denmark, Greenland, and the Faroe Islands, which are located halfway between Great Britain and Iceland.

According to the World Health Organization, 93 percent of Djibouti's female population has undergone genital circumcision, mostly performed by women in the community, and 94 percent of males have had male circumcision.

Dominica is named after the day of the week that Christopher Columbus discovered it—Sunday, which is *dominica* in Latin.

The Dominican Republic shares the island of Hispaniola with Haiti. Its capital, Santo Domingo, was the site of the first permanent European settlement in the New World.

The United States occupied the Dominican Republic from 1916 to 1924.

Today, the Dominican Republic is the top tourist destination in the Caribbean.

The only two predominantly Roman Catholic countries in Asia are East Timor (part of the island of Timor north of Australia) and the Philippines.

The summit of Mount Chimborazo in Ecuador is the farthest point on the surface from the center of the earth, due to the fact that the planet is fatter at the equator than at the latitude Mount Everest occupies.

The Galapagos Islands belong to Ecuador. The nation's largest city is Guayaquil.

Egypt lies within Africa and Asia.

El Salvador means "Republic of the Savior."

The currency of Eritrea is the nakfa.

Estonia has the highest GDP of any of the former Soviet republics.

The monarchy of Ethiopia dates back to the second century BC.

The government of Fiji was overthrown by a military coup in 2006.

France is the richest European nation and number four in the world, ranked by aggregate household wealth.

More tourists—82 million—visit France every year than any other nation in the world.

The president of Gabon is Ali Bongo Omdimba.

The currency of the Gambia is the dalasi, which equals one hundred bututs.

Germany is the largest exporter of goods in the world and the third-largest importer.

The largest artificial reservoir in the world—Lake Volta—is in Ghana.

Economy Watch ranked the economy of Ghana as the fastest growing in the world in 2011.

Greece is officially known as the Hellenic Republic.

Mount Athos in Greece has twenty Eastern Orthodox monasteries and is a self-governed autonomous region.

The tiny island nation of Grenada is one of the world's leading exporters of mace and nutmeg.

The currency of Guatemala is the quetzal, named after the national bird.

The Republic of Guinea is located in Western Africa. It is not to be confused with its neighbor Guinea-Bissau, or Equatorial Guinea, New Guinea, Papua New Guinea, or French Guiana.

Kaieteur Falls in Guyana is among the most powerful falls in the world.

Haiti became the first black-governed nation after the slave revolution in 1804. It was also the first independent country in Latin America.

Haiti is the poorest nation in the Americas.

The currency of Honduras is the lempira.

The currency of Hungary is the forint, which is named for Florence, where the coins were first minted. One forint equals one hundred fillér.

Although Iceland is close to the Arctic Circle, it has a temperate climate due to the warm Gulf Stream currents that flow past the island nation.

India is the most populous democracy in the world.

India and Pakistan have been at war with each other three times since 1947.

Indonesia is composed of 17,508 islands.

Indonesia has the world's largest Muslim population—202 million. (The next five top Islamic countries are Pakistan, India, Bangladesh, Egypt, and Nigeria.)

Iran employs seventy thousand "moral police" to ensure that men don't wear necklaces and that women don't wear their head scarves too loose, their overcoats too tight, or their pants too short.

Between 2003 and 2004, the United States sent $12 billion in cash to Iraq. The twenty-one cargo planeloads of shrink-wrapped $100 bills comprised the biggest international airlift of cash in history. In total to date, the United States has allocated more than $61 billion to help rebuild Iraq. Unfortunately, $6.6 billion of the cash has gone missing.

Ireland occupies five-sixths of the island of Ireland. Northern Ireland, which is part of the United Kingdom, occupies the rest.

Ireland seceded from the United Kingdom in 1922 and gained independence in 1931.

Israel has the highest percentage of museums per capita in the world.

The land that comprises present-day Israel has changed hands numerous times over the millennia. The area went in succession from the Kingdom of Egypt to the Hittite Empire to the Kingdom of Israel to the Assyrian Empire to the Babylonian Empire to the Persian Empire to the Macedonian Empire to the Roman Empire to the Sassanid Empire to the Caliphate to the Seljuk Empire to the Crusader States to Saladin's Empire to the Ottoman Empire to European Colonialism to the State of Israel.

Sardinia and Sicily belong to Italy.

Prior to Italy's unification in 1861, it was a collection of city-states and kingdoms.

Italy has had sixty-one governments in sixty-one years.

Jamaica is the third-largest English-speaking country in the Americas.

The characters that make up Japan's name mean "sun origin," which is why the nation is known as the "Land of the Rising Sun."

Japan is comprised of 6,852 islands.

Japan has the lowest murder rate in the world.

There are forty-seven thousand centenarians (people one hundred years old or older) in Japan.

Jordan was founded in 1921 as the Emirate of Transjordan. Today, it is known as the Hashemite Kingdom of Jordan.

Kazakhstan is the world's largest landlocked country and the ninth largest overall.

Kazakhstan's currency is the tenge, which equals one hundred tyin.

The Pacific nation of Kiribati is comprised of thirty-two atolls dispersed over 1.35 million square miles.

The average temperature high for Kuwait in August is 131°F, with an average rainfall amount of zero inches.

The Kyrgyzstan flag features a sun with forty rays and a yurt (traditional nomadic hut) inside.

The Kyrgyzstan unit of currency is the som, which is divided into one hundred tyiyn.

The currency of Laos is the kip, which is divided into one hundred at.

Laosians are divided into three main ethnic groups: the lowlanders, the midlanders, and the highlanders.

Latvia's population has decreased 15 percent since 1991.

The Latvian unit of currency is the lats.

The flag of Lebanon features a cedar tree because, in the Bible, Psalm 92:12 reads, "The righteous flourish like the palm tree, and grow like a cedar in Lebanon."

The flag of Liberia closely resembles that of the United States, with eleven red and white stripes and a blue field in the upper left corner with a large white star.

Libya, under Qaddafi, was known as the Great Socialist People's Libyan Arab Jamahiriya.

Liechtenstein is one of only two (the other being Uzbekistan) doubly landlocked countries, meaning that it is surrounded by other countries that are landlocked and one must cross the borders of two countries to reach a coast.

Liechtenstein lies entirely within the Alps.

In the fourteenth century, Lithuania was the biggest country in Europe.

The Republic of Macedonia is referred to as the former Yugoslav Republic of Macedonia by the U.N. and several countries, including Greece, who object to the other name because a region of Greece is also known as Macedonia.

Eighty percent of Madagascar's wildlife is found nowhere else in the world.

The unit of currency in Madagascar is the ariary, which is equal to five iraimbilanja. The Madagascan monetary system is one of only two in the world that are not based on a power of ten.

The unit of currency in Malawi is the kwacha, which is divided into one hundred tambala.

The Maldive Islands, although spread out over ninety thousand square miles of the Indian Ocean, constitute the smallest and least populated country in Asia.

The average height above sea level in the Maldives is just four feet, eleven inches, making it the lowest country in the world. The highest point in the country is seven feet, seven inches, the lowest high point in the world.

In 2007, only 3 percent of the people in Mali were over sixty-five.

The average woman in Mali gives birth 7.4 times.

One of the ethnic groups in Mali is the Bozo.

The unit of currency for Mauritania is the ouguiya, which is divided into five khoums.

Mauritius, a small island nation off the coast of Madagascar, was the only known home of the now extinct dodo bird.

There are thirty-one states in Mexico.

Monaco is the most densely populated country and also boasts the world's highest life expectancy—ninety. It also has the lowest unemployment rate.

Forty-five percent of Mongolia's population lives in the capital city of Ulan Bator.

Mongolia is the most sparsely populated country.

The currency of Mongolia is the tugrik. Ghenghis Khan's image adorns many denominations of money in Mongolia.

Montenegro is the newest member of the United Nations, having joined in 2006.

Montenegro means "Black Mountain." Its largest city is Podgorica.

Genetically, most Moroccans are of Berber ancestry, not Arabic.

Namibia is the second least densely populated country in the world.

In the late 1960s and early 1970s, the island nation of Nauru had the highest per capita income of any nation because of its extensive phosphate deposits. Unfortunately, rampant strip mining quickly depleted this supply and the nation became a tax haven and turned to money laundering for income.

Kathmandu is the capital of Nepal. The nation has 240 mountain peaks that are higher than twenty thousand feet.

Mount Everest, in Nepal, is so tall that it reaches into the jet stream.

The Kingdom of the Netherlands has four parts— the Netherlands, Aruba, Curaçao, and Sint Maarten.

There were no mammals in New Zealand until the arrival of humans, circa AD 1250.

The currency of Nicaragua is the córdoba.

Seventy-two percent of Niger's export proceeds come from uranium.

> Nigeria is the most populous country in Africa and the most populous nation where the majority of people are black.

Sunan International Airport in the North Korean capital of Pyongyang, the country's main airport, only gets about two or three flights a day.

> Norway gained its independence from Sweden in 1905.

As of December 2010, Norway has been ranked as the most democratic country in the world; North Korea the least democratic.

> During World War II, Norway declared itself neutral but was occupied by Germany for five years.

About 20 percent of the world's meteorite supply comes from Oman.

> Only about 1 percent of Pakistanis paid income tax in 2010. Out of a population of 170 million, just 1.9 million people filed a return.

Pakistan sends out transgendered tax collectors (men wearing makeup) to the homes and businesses of those who don't pay their taxes in order to embarrass them into doing so.

Pakistan is the only Muslim nation that has nuclear weapons.

Panama seceded from Colombia in 1903, so that the Panama Canal could be built there by the U.S. Army Corps of Engineers.

The toll rate for cruise ships over thirty thousand tons passing through the Panama Canal is based on permanent passenger beds—$92 per unoccupied berth and $115 for occupied berths.

Papua New Guinea became independent of Australia in 1975 but is still a realm of Her Majesty Elizabeth II, Queen of Papua New Guinea.

Paraguay has two official languages—Spanish and Guarani. The currency of Paraguay is also called the guarani.

The president of Peru from 1990 to 2000 was Alberto Fujimori, whose parents emigrated from Japan.

The Philippines consist of 7,170 islands.

The Philippines are named after King Philip II of Spain.

The Kingdom of Poland was formed in 1025.

The zloty is the currency of Poland. It is divided into one hundred groszy.

Portugal established the world's first truly global empire and was the longest lasting of the European Colonial empires.

Qatar had the world's highest GDP per capita in 2010.

Women are outnumbered two to one in Qatar, where many South Asian men migrate to work.

The name "Romania" derives from the Latin *romanus*, meaning "citizen of Rome."

Russia spans nine time zones and contains one-eighth of the world's populated landmass.

Russia recognizes twenty-one different ethic minorities within its borders.

The three cultural groups in Rwanda are the Hutu, Tutsi, and Twa.

Samoa used to be known as Western Samoa and German Samoa.

Samoan men get intricate geometrical tattoos called *pe'a* that extend from the knees up to the ribs. The women get tattoos called *malu* that start just below the knees and extend to the upper thighs.

The tiny nation of San Marino, which is surrounded by Italy, is also called the Most Serene Republic of San Marino.

San Marino is the oldest sovereign state in the world, having its roots in a monastic community begun in 301.

San Marino also boasts the oldest continuous constitution, enacted in 1600.

San Marino has no national debt.

Abdul-Aziz bin Saud founded the absolute monarchy of Saudi Arabia in 1932, which his family has ruled ever since.

Saudi Arabia is the biggest country in the Middle East.

Since 1985, Saudi Arabia has demolished about 95 percent of Mecca's historic buildings dating back to the time of Mohammed, as they fear worship of a building will lead to idolatry. Five mosques built by Mohammed's daughter have been bulldozed, as well as his wife's house, which now is the site of public restrooms.

Thirteen million people a year visit Mecca. The city is closed to all but Muslims.

Ten percent of Serbia's land is national parks.

The most common language in Sierra Leone is Krio, which is an amalgam of English and several different indigenous languages.

Singapore is the second most densely populated country, after Monaco.

Forty-three percent of Singapore's population is foreigners.

English is the most commonly spoken language in Singapore.

In 2010, Singapore had the world's fastest-growing economy.

Only 30 percent of Somalis have access to clean drinking water.

Somalia has the longest coastline of any African nation.

Samosas, three-sided minced meat and vegetable pastry treats, have been banned in Somalia because the Muslim authorities there feel the three sides represent the Trinity.

South Africa has eleven official languages—Afrikaans, English, IsiNdebele, IsiXhosa, IsiZulu, Sesotho, Sesotho sa Leboa, Setswana, siSwati, Tshivenda, and Xitsonga.

South Africa is the first African nation to permit same-sex marriages. Eighty percent of the population is Christian.

It is believed that one in thirty-eight South Korean children is autistic.

The world's newest country is South Sudan, which gained independence from Sudan in 2011.

Spain ceded Gibraltar to Britain in 1713 after the War of Spanish Succession. Spain today lays claim to this British territory, although the citizens of Gibraltar have repeatedly voted down referenda to return to Spanish sovereignty.

Cinnamon is native to Sri Lanka.

Suriname, which lies on the northern coast, is the smallest country in South America.

Swaziland has the highest rate of HIV infection in the world. More than 50 percent of people in their twenties are afflicted.

The currency of Swaziland is the lilangeni.

The second-largest city in Sweden is Göteborg.

Sweden has not been at war since 1814, longer than Switzerland.

Switzerland had the highest wealth per person of any country in the world in 2010.

Switzerland is not a member of the European Union.

The Palace of Nations, the second-largest United Nations center, is in Geneva, Switzerland.

Syria suspended its constitution and has been under "emergency law" since 1963.

The currency of Tajikistan is the somoni, which is subdivided into one hundred diram.

Tanzania gets its name from Tanganyika and Zanzibar, which joined together in 1964.

Thailand is the kingdom that has had the most different reigns in world history, although King Rama IX has ruled the nation since 1946, making him the longest-sitting monarch in the world as of 2011.

Prostitution is illegal in Thailand, although there are an estimated three hundred thousand prostitutes involved in the flourishing trade, and the business makes up about 3 percent of the country's economy.

The currency of Thailand is the baht, which is subdivided into one hundred satang.

In the Tiwi tribe of the Tiwi Islands that lie just north of Australia, all females must be married at all times. Thus, girls are married at birth to men at least sixty years old. The girls do not live with their elderly husbands until they turn fourteen.

From the 1500s to the 1700s, Togo had such a thriving slave trade that it was known as the "Slave Coast."

The currency of Tonga is the pa'anga, which is subdivided into one hundred seniti.

Trinidad and Tobago is the birthplace of steel drums, the limbo, and calypso.

Trinidad is nineteen times bigger than its sister island of Tobago.

Tunisia is Africa's northernmost country.

Ninety-seven percent of Turkey is in Asia, 3 percent is in Europe.

Turkey is one of six Turkic states, the other five being Azerbaijan, Kazakhstan, Kyrgyzstan, Turkmenistan, and Uzbekistan.

Seventy percent of Turkmenistan is covered by the Kara-Kum (Black Sand) desert.

Turkmenistan has the fourth-largest natural gas reserves in the world.

Eighty-four percent of Uganda's population is Christian.

Homosexuality is illegal in Uganda.

Ukraine is the largest country entirely within Europe.

Ukraine has the second-biggest armed forces in Europe, after Russia.

The United Arab Emirates is comprised of seven emirates—Muslim territories ruled by an emir—

two of which are Dubai and Abu Dhabi. Each emir has absolute power over his emirate.

There is an $11 million Christmas tree in the lobby of the Emirates Palace Hotel in Abu Dhabi. It is decorated with gold and jewel-studded ornaments.

The British Empire was at its height in 1922.

The United Kingdom still has fourteen overseas territories.

The English royal estate at Balmoral Castle in Scotland comprises forty-nine thousand acres.

While English is the official language of the United Kingdom, there are several regional languages, including Cornish, Gaelic, Irish, Scots, Scottish, and Ulster Scots.

Eighty-eight percent of Uruguay's population is of European descent.

Uruguay was the first country in the world to give every schoolchild a free laptop and Wi-Fi.

The Aral Sea, which Uzbekistan shares with Kazakhstan, was once the fourth-largest lake in the world. Due to the Soviet Union diverting the rivers that feed it to grow cotton, the lake was just 10 percent of its original size by 2007 and now has split into three small lakes.

The currency of Vanuatu, a Pacific island nation, is the vatu, which has no subunits.

Venezuela is officially known as the Bolivarian Republic of Venezuela.

Vietnam is the thirteenth most populous country.

Vietnam gained independence from China in 938.

Forty-six percent of the population in Yemen is under fifteen, while only 2.7 percent is over sixty-five.

Leaves of the khat plant are chewed by Yemenis in the afternoon for their stimulative effect. Khat is also commonly chewed during business negotiations, to aid in decision making.

Zambia was known as Northern Rhodesia while under British rule.

The name "Zambia" comes from the Zambezi River.

The currency of Zambia is the kwacha, which is subdivided into one hundred ngwee.

Zimbabwe has no national currency. It was suspended due to hyperinflation, and official business is conducted with U.S. dollars.

Zimbabwe is the country with the highest rate of death from infectious diseases, followed by Zambia, Swaziland, Botswana, and Malawi.

ALMA MATTERS

Yale University began as the Collegiate School, which trained clergy and politicians. The school was renamed Yale in 1718 after a monetary gift from Elihu Yale, a governor of the British East India Company.

> Yale was the first American school to offer a PhD, in 1861.

Dartmouth is the smallest school in the Ivy League.

> Dartmouth began as Moor's Indian Charity School, which was founded in 1755 to Christianize Native Americans in Connecticut. After the school moved to New Hampshire in 1769, it was renamed Dartmouth, for William Legge, Second Earl of Dartmouth, who was a supporter of the Charity School but ironically was opposed to supporting his namesake college.

Rutgers University was founded by the Dutch Reformed Church as Queens College in 1766 to train future ministers. Queens College shut its doors after the War of 1812, due to lack of funds. It reopened in 1825, after a donation from American Revolution hero Colonel Henry Rutgers.

> Temple University has its roots in night classes taught by Russell Conwell, a Baptist minister, in the basement of Philadelphia's Grace Baptist Church. It was known as Conwell's Baptist Temple and the students were known as "night owls." Hence the origin of the school's team name—the Owls.

William of Orange was a Dutchman known as King William III, who ruled England, Ireland, and Scotland from 1689 to 1702. Part of his reign was shared with his wife Mary II. They chartered William and Mary College in 1693.

GOOD WORK, IF YOU CAN GET IT

A U.S. federal employee has a greater chance of dying from natural causes than of getting fired. Death is the primary threat to job security for workers at more than a dozen big government agencies. In 2010, of the 1,832 employees at the Federal Communications Commission and the 1,189 at the Federal Trade Commission, exactly zero were fired or laid off.

NEVER NEEDS REPLACING

The longest continuously burning lightbulb is in the Livermore-Pleasantville Fire Department in Livermore,

California. The sixty-watt bulb has been lit constantly (except for a one-week period in 1937 when the building was being renovated) since 1901.

The oldest operating electric signs in the United States are located in the Ocean Grove Camp Meeting Association Building in Ocean Grove, New Jersey. One says "Holiest to the Lord," and another says "So Be Ye Holy."

IS THAT LEGAL?

Liquor sales are illegal on Sundays in fourteen states.

In Utah, it is illegal for a new restaurant to allow patrons to be able to see bartenders or their drinks being prepared. So-called Zion curtains, state-mandated partitions, must be installed between the bar and customers.

In forty-three states it is legal to openly carry firearms, with the proper permits.

Four states—Alaska, Hawaii, Maine, and Vermont— prohibit outdoor billboards along their roadways.

Fireworks are banned in four states—Delaware, Massachusetts, New Jersey, and New York.

In Pennsylvania, which borders three of the four fireworks-banned states, the sale of high-explosive aerial fireworks and other kinds that are illegal in

Pennsylvania are allowed for non-Pennsylvania residents. As a result, there are numerous fireworks stores lining the Pennsylvania side of the borders with these states.

LONE STAR POWER

The United States has three power grids—one in the East, one in the West, and one for the state of Texas.

Texas is the number one wind power–producing state.

The Texas state capitol is fifteen feet taller than the U.S. Capitol.

SLITHERIN'

The annual rattlesnake roundup in Sweetwater, Texas, draws thirty to fifty thousand visitors each year, where they catch and kill as many snakes as possible.

The event hosts a Miss Snake Charmer pageant, where young ladies skin and decapitate rattlesnakes with a machete.

For ten dollars visitors can also skin a snake, rub their hands in the blood, and put their handprints on a wall to mark their achievement.

GOOD HANDS?

Mississippi leads the nation in uninsured drivers, with 28 percent. Following close behind are New Mexico with 26 percent and Tennessee with 24 percent.

Maine and Massachusetts have the lowest rate of uninsured drivers at just 4.5 percent, followed by New York at 5 percent.

FAITH NO MORE

A 2011 Gallup poll found that Mississippi is the most religious state and that Vermont is the least religious.

There are 250,000 Amish in America, spread out over twenty-eight states.

Eighty percent of Utah's state legislators are Mormons.

WATER WISE

Forty percent of the water in the continental United States drains into the Mississippi River.

According to the Natural Resources Defense Council, the cleanest beach water in the United States, when it comes to bacterial contamination, is at Rehoboth Beach and Dewey Beach in Delaware. Overall, New Hampshire is the state with the cleanest beach water, followed by New Jersey. Of course, New Hampshire has the shortest ocean coastline in America, at just 18 miles. New Jersey's coastline is 130 miles long.

The worst beach water is found at Avalon Beach in Los Angeles; Ropes Park in Nueces County Texas; and Keaton Beach in Taylor County, Florida.

Revere Beach, in Revere, Massachusetts, was founded in 1895 and is America's oldest public beach.

The main reason Hoover Dam was built was for flood control. Its secondary functions are water storage and power generation.

With a depth of 1,645 feet, Lake Tahoe is the second-deepest lake in the United States, after Crater Lake, which is 1,945 feet deep.

Florida is the state that spends the most each year on boats and boating accessories, followed by Texas, New York, North Carolina, and Louisiana.

PLATE PASSION

New York was the first state to require license plates, in 1901; however, the state did not supply them and motorists had to make their own. West Virginia and Massachusetts were the first states to issue them, in 1903.

Some Native American Indian tribal nations issue their own plates.

Nineteen states only require a rear license plate.

Low-number plates are highly sought after in Delaware, and the state allows the reselling of plates.

Three-digit plates sell in the range of $50,000 on the secondary license plate market, while two-digit plates can go for up to $200,000. In 2008, Delaware license plate number "6" sold for $675,000.

One in ten drivers in California has a handicapped placard.

🌰 VANITY, THY NAME IS VIRGINIA

There are 9.3 million vehicles with vanity license plates in the United States. Virginia has 10 percent of them. Sixteen percent of vehicles in Virginia sport vanity plates.

New Hampshire, Illinois, Nevada, and Montana round out the top five vanity plate–loving states. Texas has the fewest; just one-half of 1 percent of vehicles have vanity plates in the Lone Star State.

NEXT EXIT 49 MILES

The farthest distance between two exits on any interstate highway is the forty-nine miles from Yeehaw Junction/Exit 193 to Kissimmee St. Cloud/Exit 242 on the northbound lanes of Florida's Turnpike.

State Highway M-185 on Mackinac Island in Michigan is the only state highway in the country that does not allow motor vehicles.

BOTTOMS UP

North Dakota leads the country in binge drinking, that is, five or more drinks on one occasion, with 30 percent of those older than twelve doing so in a month. Utah has the lowest percentage of binge drinkers, with 14 percent per month.

> Vermont leads the nation in underage drinking, with 36.6 percent of twelve- to twenty-year-olds admitting to drinking in an average month. Utah comes in last in that department, with 14 percent.

Alaska has the highest rate of illegal drug usage, with 13.5 percent of people over the age of twelve reporting doing so per month. Iowa the lowest, with 5.3 percent.

> Kentucky has the highest percentage of people who smoke cigarettes per month, with 32 percent, and Utah has the lowest, with 16.4 percent.

Wyoming is the state with the highest percentage of tobacco chewers. One in six men in Wyoming do so, as does 9 percent of the overall population, including women.

RELAX

Portfolio.com ranked Detroit as the most stressful city to live in. Salt Lake City was ranked least stressful.

FLAGGING INTEREST

Three different university studies all found that the mere glimpse of an American flag was enough to bias people to vote for Republicans, even several days after having viewed one.

The state of South Carolina still flies the Confederate battle flag at its statehouse.

QUAKER STATE

For thirty years, Pennsylvania was the world's leading producer of oil.

The world's oldest continually producing oil well is McClintock Well No. 1, located in northwestern Pennsylvania. It was drilled in 1861.

Pennsylvania's oil heritage can be seen today in the oil company names Quaker State and Pennzoil.

MONEY MATTERS

U.S. banknotes (bills) that are found to have been incorrectly printed are pulled from circulation and destroyed. They are substituted with a replacement note bearing the same serial number with a small green star at the end.

The series year found on a banknote indicates the year that that bill design was introduced, not the year of the note itself.

Today's notes have a bright green seal. Some earlier notes also may have had an orange seal, meaning they were Gold Certificates and could be redeemed for their value in gold coins, up until 1934. Notes with blue seals were Silver Certificates and could have been redeemed for silver coins up until 1964, or silver bullion up until 1968.

> The United States stores its vast gold reserves in several locations, including Fort Knox, Kentucky; the Federal Reserve Bank in Manhattan; West Point, New York; and Denver, Colorado.

Lottery winnings are not considered income by the U.S. government when determining federal aid. A Michigan man won $2 million in the lottery and was able to continue to receive food stamps.

> Illinois, "The Land of Lincoln," is the only state where toll roads accept pennies in their automatic toll lanes.

Each year, most Alaska residents receive large checks for their share of the state's vast oil wealth. In 2011, the state sent out checks for $1,174 each.

BONDAGE

The United States still holds debt from the Revolutionary War. Many government-issued bonds from that time period went unredeemed.

There are currently $16 billion worth of U.S. savings bonds issued that have reached maturity and are no longer earning interest.

COUNTY NEWS

The county with the highest property taxes in the United States is Hunterdon County, New Jersey, followed by Nassau County, New York; Westchester County, New York; Bergen County, New Jersey; and Rockland County, New York.

> Texas County, Missouri, is the center of population in the United States. This is the point on the map from which an equal number of Americans live in any direction.

Canadian County is in Oklahoma.

LOCATION, LOCATION, LOCATION

The American street with the highest cost to rent office space is Sand Hill Road in Menlo Park, California, followed by Fifth Avenue, New York; Greenwich Avenue, Greenwich, Connecticut; University Avenue, Palo Alto, California; and Pennsylvania Avenue, Washington, DC.

GOING POSTAL

United States Postal Service workers are not employed by the federal government.

> More letter carriers are attacked by dogs in May than any other month. The fewest letter carriers are attacked in January.

USELESS STATS

Medicaid denies coverage to men who have breast cancer.

The bedrock underneath New York City contains opals.

The highest sea cliffs in the world are located at Kalaupapa, Hawaii, on the island of Molokai. They rise 3,315 feet above the Pacific Ocean.

To become a state, a territory must have a population of at least sixty thousand, a constitution, and proposed borders.

Akron, Ohio, used to bill itself as the "Bowling Capital of the World."

The western United States received so much snowfall in the 2010–11 winter season that several ski resorts were able to remain open for business until July 4, including Squaw Valley, California, which received over eight hundred inches of the white stuff.

The town of Scenic, South Dakota, went on sale in 2011. The asking price for the twelve-acre town with a population under ten was $799,000.

Thirty percent of Americans surveyed say it takes them more than ninety minutes to mow their lawns.

"FIRST" FLIGHTS

Teddy Roosevelt was the first president to fly in an aircraft. He did so in 1910, in a Wright Flyer, after he had left office.

Any airplane that the president is on is technically considered "Air Force One."

The 747s that serve the president are only called Air Force One after he sets foot on the plane.

The two planes commonly associated with being Air Force One are Boeing VC-25 versions of the Boeing 747.

The two official planes that usually serve as Air Force One have fifty-three antennae for the multiple forms of communications on board.

The two Air Force One planes are dismantled every so often and reassembled following security sweeps.

There are three presidential helicopters, known as Marine One. The commander in chief travels on one and the other two fly with it as decoys.

Dwight D. Eisenhower was the first president to ride in a helicopter in 1957.

"FIRST" FACTS

Jimmy Carter shot his younger sister Gloria in the behind with a BB gun as a boy.

Bill Clinton was born William Jefferson Blythe III. His father died in a car wreck three months before he was born. At age fourteen, he adopted the last name of his stepfather, Roger Clinton.

President Harry Truman was broke when he left office. He was offered deals to put his name on products like soap and clothing stores. He wrote a book instead.

President Gerald Ford was so despondent after losing the 1976 election to Jimmy Carter that he contemplated suicide, believing Carter to be a far inferior choice.

President George Herbert Walker Bush had never seen a price code scanner in person until ten years after they came into general use.

Richard Nixon fancied cottage cheese.

George W. Bush disliked fish.

Grover Cleveland was born in New Jersey, but he was distantly related to General Moses Cleveland, whom Cleveland, Ohio, was named for.

Rutherford B. Hayes had the first presidential yacht.

Presidents had yachts up until Jimmy Carter sold the USS *Sequoia*.

William McKinley was the first president to ride in an automobile—a Stanley Steamer, in 1899.

After JFK was assassinated in the back of his limo, the car was retrofitted at a cost of $1 million to make it more secure. This limo stayed in use until Jimmy Carter's term.

James Buchanan is the only president from Pennsylvania.

Franklin Pierce is the only president from New Hampshire.

Seven of the eleven presidents elected from 1869 to 1921 were from Ohio. They were Ulysses S. Grant, Rutherford B. Hayes, James Garfield, Benjamin Harrison, William McKinley, William Howard Taft, and Warren G. Harding.

The name "Barack" is of African origin and means "blessed."

Bill Clinton has made $60 million in speaking fees since he left office.

Ronald Reagan's eyesight was so bad that he was not eligible for combat duty during World War II. He acted in propaganda films instead.

Ronald Reagan lost half of his blood when he was shot in 1981, despite arriving at the hospital within five minutes.

The Secret Service code name for Reagan was "Rawhide." Nancy Reagan's code name was "Rainbow."

Reagan once starred in a movie about the Secret Service.

HE'S AN EXCELLENT DRIVER

As of 2011, President Obama had only driven a car twice in the previous four years. On one of those occasions he only drove ten feet.

SPEAKING OF PRESIDENTS

Thomas Jefferson was fluent in French, Greek, Italian, Latin, and Spanish.

John Adams was fluent in French, Greek, Hebrew, and Latin.

John Quincy Adams was fluent in French, German, and Latin, and conversational in Dutch and Greek.

Martin Van Buren spoke English as a second language. Although born in America, Dutch was his primary language.

James Garfield was fluent in Greek and Latin and also ambidextrous. He would entertain friends by writing answers to questions in Greek with one hand and Latin with the other, simultaneously.

Herbert Hoover was fluent in Mandarin Chinese.

Barack Obama is conversational in Indonesian.

MASTER GEORGE

George Washington became a slave owner at age eleven. He went on to own three hundred slaves.

Washington bought teeth from his slaves to supplement his dentures.

While Washington was president, one of his female slaves escaped and he conspired to have her kidnapped and returned.

Although Washington believed slavery was wrong, he couldn't bring himself to set his free. His will specified that they would be set free and educated upon his death and that of his wife, Martha. When George died before Martha, she set their slaves free, fearing that they would kill her to gain their freedom.

HONESTLY ABE

Abraham Lincoln moved to Illinois ("The Land of Lincoln") when he was twenty-eight.

An assassination attempt on Lincoln's life was thwarted just before his first inauguration.

THE POOR HOUSE

In the early days, the executive branch was poorly funded to keep the president from gaining too much power.

Thomas Jefferson had to hire his own secretary.

Grover Cleveland had to answer the White House phone himself.

People used to picnic on the White House lawn.

HIPPITY-HOP

The annual Easter Egg Roll on the South Lawn of the White House was inaugurated by the administration of Rutherford B. Hayes in 1878. Before this, it took place on the grounds of the U.S. Capitol, until lawmakers banished the event because of the mess it left behind.

CLOSE CALLS

There were ninety-one breaches of White House security between 1980 and 2003.

In 1993, a car-bomb attempt on the life of ex-president George H. W. Bush was foiled in Kuwait, where he gave a speech.

In 1994, a man fired twenty-nine shots at the White House, trying to kill Bill Clinton.

Also in 1994, a man tried to fly a Cessna plane into the White House, only to end up crashing on the White House lawn.

Early on the morning of September 11, 2001, a van loaded with Middle Eastern men arrived at the hotel President George W. Bush was staying at on Longboat Key, Florida, insisting that they had an interview with him. They were turned away. Two days earlier, a similar ploy was used to assassinate an anti-Taliban leader in Afghanistan.

In 2005, while President Bush was making an address in Tbilisi, Georgia, a man threw a live grenade at him, which failed to explode.

CHURCH AND STATE

There are 304 Protestant members in the U.S. Congress, 156 Catholics, 39 Jews, 15 Mormons, 15 "other," and 6 unknowns.

Joe Biden is the first Catholic to serve as vice president.

HAPPY CAMPERS

Camp David—the presidential retreat—is officially known as Naval Support Facility Thurmont.

Camp David was built as a camp for federal agents and their families in 1938, sixty miles north of Washington, DC, in rural Maryland.

FDR made the camp a presidential retreat in 1942 and called it Shangri-La.

Dwight D. Eisenhower renamed it Camp David to honor his grandson David.

Ronald Reagan is the president who spent the most time at Camp David.

The camp's Evergreen Chapel is Barack Obama's primary place of worship.

Camp David is so secretive and remote that it doesn't appear on local maps of the area.

HOUSTON, WE HAVE A PROBLEM

In 2005, Texas congresswoman Sheila Jackson Lee famously asked NASA if the *Mars Pathfinder* had taken an image of the flag Neil Armstrong planted on Mars. At the time, Lee represented the Houston area and was a member of the House Science Committee's space subcommittee. In 2010, Lee noted, "Today we have two Vietnams, side by side, North and South, exchanging and working." (Vietnam has been one country since 1976.) She served on the House Foreign Affairs Committee at the time.

Several other prominent politicians are guilty of not engaging their brains before opening their mouths. Some choice examples follow:

GEORGE W. BUSH

"Families is where our nation finds hope, where wings take dream."

"We got issue in America. Too many good docs [doctors] are getting out of business. Too many good OB-GYNs aren't able to practice their, their love with women across the country."

"You teach a child to read, and he or her will be able to pass a literacy test."

"They misunderestimated me."

"Rarely is the question asked: Is our children learning?"

"Our enemies are innovative and resourceful, and so are we. They never stop thinking about new ways to harm our country and our people, and neither do we."

"Africa is a nation that suffers from incredible disease."

DAN QUAYLE

"I love California, I practically grew up in Phoenix."

BARACK OBAMA

"Over the past fifteen months, we've traveled to every corner of the United States. I've now been in fifty-seven states? I think one left to go."

TIM KAINE

"Well, first, Joe [Biden] comes from a state, Delaware, that borders Virginia." (These states do not share a border.)

JOE BIDEN

"A man I'm proud to call my friend. A man who will be the next President of the United States—Barack America."

"I mean you got the first mainstream African American who is articulate and bright and clean and a nice-looking guy."

"A successful dump!" (proclaimed to the press after depositing wood at the local landfill)

"You cannot go to a 7-Eleven or Dunkin' Donuts unless you have a slight Indian accent . . . I'm not joking."

". . . the number one job facing the middle class . . . a three-letter word, jobs, J-O-B-S."

"Stand up, Chuck, let 'em see ya." (said to wheelchair-bound Missouri state senator Chuck Graham)

NANCY PELOSI

"Every month we don't have an economic recovery package 500 million Americans lose their jobs."

"But we have to pass the [health care] bill so that you can find out what's in it . . ."

HARRY REID

"Only thirty-six thousand people lost their jobs today, which is a good thing."

"Without the auto bailout, there would be no Ford today." (Ford did not take any bailout money.)

WHITE MEN'S CLUB

Hiram Rhodes Revels was the first black man ever elected to the U.S. Senate, in 1870. Fittingly, he filled Confederate president Jefferson Davis's old seat from Mississippi. Revels remains today one of only six African Americans to ever serve in the U.S. Senate.

FIRST HALF SISTER

Barack Obama's half sister is Maya Kasandra Soetoro-Ng. She was named after Maya Angelou.

Obama lived with Soetoro-Ng for several years in Indonesia and Hawaii when they were children.

Soetoro-Ng has a half sister, Rahayu Nurmaido Soetoro, and a half brother, Yusuf Aji Soetoro, from her father's second marriage.

PORNO DIPLOMACY

Secretary of State Hillary Clinton's former intern—Sammie Spades—became a porn star.

IT TAKES A STRONG CONSTITUTION

The U.S. Constitution was never signed by John Adams or Thomas Jefferson, since Adams was overseas serving as U.S. minister to Great Britain and Jefferson was serving as minister to France at the time of the Constitutional Convention.

Benjamin Franklin was old and in poor health and needed help to sign the document.

The Constitution was "penned" by Jacob Shallus, a Pennsylvania General Assembly clerk, for thirty dollars.

Three of the forty-two delegates to the convention—Eldridge Gerry, Edmund Randolph, and George Mason—refused to sign the Constitution because it did not include a Bill of Rights.

The Constitution is on display at the National Archives Building in Washington, DC. Its four pages are protected in an argon gas–filled titanium case kept at 67°F and 40 percent relative humidity.

O SAY CAN YOU SEE . . .

The national anthem may have been written in the form of a poem by Francis Scott Key in 1814, but it was not officially recognized as the nation's anthem until Congress did so in 1931. Before this, songs like "My Country, 'Tis of Thee" and "Hail Columbia" were often used at official functions.

I PLEDGE ALLEGIENCE . . .

The Pledge of Allegiance was written by Francis Bellamy, a Christian Socialist, in 1892, in support of a flag promotion being run by the nation's largest circulation publication of the time—*Youth's Companion.*

> The goal of the campaign was to get an American flag in every school in the country. Bellamy's pledge was to be recited and accompanied by the Bellamy Salute, which involved extending the arm straight out. This salute was discontinued at the outbreak of World War II, because it resembled the Nazi salute, and was replaced by placing the right hand over the heart.

Bellamy's original pledge was, "I pledge allegiance to *my* Flag and to the Republic for which it stands, one nation, indivisible, with liberty and justice for all."

> President Eisenhower persuaded Congress to add the words "under God" in 1954 because of the threat of secular communism.

MARY HAD A LITTLE PROBLEM

Mary Lincoln was the first president's wife to be called "First Lady." The term was coined by a British journalist of the time.

> Since Mary was from Kentucky, which was a border state that allowed slavery during the Civil War, Southerners thought her a traitor and Northerners were very suspicious of her.

Two of Mary Lincoln's brothers were killed fighting for the Confederates during the Civil War.

> Mary was a compulsive shopper and is believed to have been bipolar.

After Abraham Lincoln's death, Mary walked around with $56,000 worth of war bonds sewn into her petticoats.

> Mary's nephew, William L. Todd, designed the first Bear Flag, the California state flag.

ANNUAL ADDRESS

The U.S. Constitution (Article II, Section 3) decrees that the president must "from time to time give to Congress Information of the State of the Union and recommend to their Consideration such Measures as he shall judge to be necessary and expedient."

George Washington gave the first State of the Union message in 1790. It lasted only about ten minutes.

In his 1823 message, James Monroe issued a warning to European powers to avoid intervention in the affairs of North and South America. This came to be known as the Monroe Doctrine.

Lincoln used his 1862 address to express his desire to free the slaves.

The first State of the Union address to be aired on radio was that of Calvin Coolidge in 1923. Harry Truman's 1947 address was the first to be televised. LBJ's 1965 address was the first delivered in prime time, not at midday as had been the usual practice.

CAPITOL IDEA

The Statue of Liberty could fit inside the rotunda of the Capitol building.

The Capitol was built using slave labor, as was the White House.

RIDDLE ME THIS

In 1990, a $250,000 sculpture named Kryptos was erected on the grounds of the Central Intelligence Agency headquarters in Langley, Virginia. The piece contains four sections of encrypted text that creator Jim Sanborn included to amuse CIA workers and others interested in cryptograms. The solution to the puzzles was given to CIA director William Webster for safekeeping. As of 2011, three of the four sections had been solved.

CAPITAL BY DESIGN

Washington, DC, is the only capital city to have been specifically built as such.

PERSONALITY PAGE

OSAMA BIN HIDIN'

Osama bin Laden's full name was Osama bin Mohammed Awad bin Laden.

His mother was the tenth wife of his father—Mohammed bin Laden—who made $5 billion in the construction business.

At the age of thirteen, Osama bin Laden inherited $80 million when his father died in a helicopter crash.

One of bin Laden's hobbies was writing poetry.

Bin Laden had twenty-three children with him in his compound at the time of his death. They may have been there to discourage an American air strike.

According to family members, bin Laden made his wives and children live without refrigerators or air-conditioning.

Bin Laden let his fighters experiment with poison gases on his family dogs.

HELLO DALAI

The name "Dalai Lama" is from the Mongolian *dalai*, meaning "ocean," and the Tibetan word *bla-ma*, meaning "high priest."

> The Dalai Lama is believed by his Buddhist follow-ers to be the reincarnation of one in a long line of manifestations of the bodhisattva (spiritual leader) of compassion who have chosen to be reborn to en-lighten others.

The present Dalai Lama is number fourteen in the succession, which dates back to 1391.

DAPPER DICTATOR

Muammar Qaddafi was a clothes horse, who changed outfits several times a day.

> Qaddafi's son, Al-Saadi Qaddafi, is a movie producer. Another of Qaddafi's sons, Muatassim, has hired Mariah Carey, Usher, and Beyoncé to perform for him. (Beyoncé and Carey ended up returning the money they were paid.)

Ugandan dictator Idi Amin once married one of Qad-dafi's daughters.

Qaddafi was thought to be worth $70 billion.

Qaddafi's private security contingent was called the Amazonia Guard. It was comprised of about forty virgins handpicked by the dictator.

Qaddafi kept five Ukrainian nurses on staff, who called him "Daddy." He never traveled without his personal nurse, a voluptuous Ukrainian blond named Halyna Kolotnytska.

Every September 1 Qaddafi gave expensive watches and medallions featuring his image to those in his entourage.

Qaddafi apparently had a crush on former U.S. secretary of state Condoleezza Rice. When his compound in Tripoli was overrun by rebel fighters, they found a photo album dedicated to her. He once stated that he "loved her very much."

DR. SCHLOMO

Sigmund Freud, born Sigismund Schlomo Freud, was a neurologist, not a psychologist.

Freud once spent a month dissecting hundreds of eels, trying to find the male reproductive organs. He failed.

Freud is reported to have had an affair with his sister-in-law.

Freud advocated cocaine for the treatment of various mental disorders and was a user himself.

FLY LIKE AN EAGLE

Many boys who became Eagle Scouts went on to reach great heights later in life, including Neil Armstrong, Marion Barry, Michael Bloomberg, Gerald Ford, L. Ron Hubbard, Alfred Kinsey, Michael Moore, Ozzie Nelson, Ross Perot, Donald Rumsfeld, and Steven Spielberg.

SHORT STOP

J. Edgar Hoover was so short, at five foot seven, that he shortened the legs of all the other chairs in his office so that he would appear taller to his visitors.

Attila the Hun was also very short and is said to have needed help to get on his horse.

FOREIGN IMPORTS

Napoléon Bonaparte was Corsican, not French. He didn't even begin to learn French until he was nine years old.

St. Patrick was not Irish. He was born in Britain and kidnapped into slavery by Irish raiders when he was around sixteen. After six years, he escaped back to England. He returned to Ireland after becoming a bishop in the church.

St. Patrick did not banish all the snakes from Ireland, as the island never had any.

Adolf Hitler was Austrian, not German. He spoke with a pronounced Austrian accent.

Josef Stalin was Georgian, not Russian. He spoke Georgian until beginning to learn to speak Russian at age ten, when he went into the seminary.

BRIGHT IDEAS

Thomas Edison did not invent the lightbulb, but he did perfect it.

Edison attended school for just three months. He was then homeschooled by his mother.

Edison was known as the "Wizard of Menlo Park." He left Menlo Park, New Jersey, in 1886 and moved his laboratories to West Orange, New Jersey. Menlo Park changed its name to Edison, New Jersey, in 1954.

A young Edison claimed to have read every book in the Detroit Public Library.

Edison went deaf as a young man.

Edison founded fourteen different companies, including General Electric.

Two of Edison's children were nicknamed "Dash" and "Dot" in recognition of his early job working as a telegraph operator.

Edison's son Charles became governor of New Jersey and his son Theodore had more than eighty patents.

The first motion picture to tell a complete story was the twelve-minute-long *The Great Train Robbery*, shot by Edison Studios in 1903.

ONE DAY AT A TIME

Alcoholics Anonymous (AA) was cofounded by William "Bill" Wilson after he had a spiritual revelation while in rehab in 1934.

> In the 1950s, Wilson experimented with using LSD to cure alcoholism. He was joined in this by *Brave New World* author Aldous Huxley, who was so fond of the drug that he requested some on his deathbed, just before passing away.

Wilson also believed in spiritualism and that a fifteenth-century monk named Boniface was guiding him during the writing of his twelve-step program to kick booze.

> While Wilson never had another drink after his religious experience, he remained a lifelong smoker, who died from emphysema, even continuing to smoke while hooked up to oxygen tanks in his final days.

Today, AA has more than 2 million members in more than one hundred thousand local groups around the world.

LEATHERNECK AND LACE

Brigadier General Loretta Reynolds became the first female commander of the Marine training facility at Parris Island, South Carolina, in 2011.

KING OF SCOTLAND

Ugandan dictator Idi Amin once served as an assistant cook in the British Colonial Army.

Amin declared himself "the uncrowned King of Scotland" in 1976. He entertained visiting dignitaries with bagpipe music and dressed in kilts.

In 1977, Amin bestowed upon himself the title of "his excellency President for Life, Field Marshal Al Hadji Doctor Idi Amin, VC, DSO, MC, Lord of All the Beasts of the Earth and Fishes of the Sea and Conqueror of the British Empire in Africa in General and Uganda in Particular."

REQUIRED READING

Mao Zedong was once an assistant librarian at Peking University.

Mao was a chain smoker who rarely got out of bed later in life.

Mao had a string of sexual partners, many of whom gave him venereal diseases.

Mao never bathed or brushed his teeth.

Quotations from Chairman Mao Tse-Tung, also known as "The Little Red Book," was required reading for all students and workers in China during the Cultural Revolution. It is estimated that about 1 billion copies were printed.

IT'S NOT ROCKET SCIENCE

Albert Einstein was offered the presidency of Israel when that nation was founded, but he declined.

"TROUBLEMAKER"

Nelson Mandela was born Rolihlahla Mandela. When he attended school as a child, his teacher gave him the English name Nelson. Rolihlahla means "to pull a branch of a tree" or, colloquially, "troublemaker."

Mandela has been married three times and has six children and twenty grandchildren.

Mandela's third wife, Graça Machel, is the widow of the former president of Mozambique. Machel is the only woman in history to have been the first lady of two different countries.

ALL IN THE FAMILY

FDR and Winston Churchill were eighth cousins.

MICKEY MOUSE EMPEROR

Japanese emperor Hirohito, who ordered the invasion of China in 1937, resulting in the Rape of Nanking, where an estimated three hundred thousand men, women, and children were murdered and/or raped, was buried with his Mickey Mouse watch.

VIVA LA REVOLUCION!

Che Guevara, who was second in command during the Cuban Revolution, was born in Argentina. His father was of Irish descent, with the last name Lynch.

Guevara studied medicine.

Guevara was in charge of the firing squads used to execute war criminals after the revolution.

Guevara left Cuba in 1965 to fight revolutions in other countries, including the Congo and Bolivia, where he was captured and executed in 1967. His hands were cut off and sent to Argentina for fingerprint verification and later to Cuba.

Simón José Antonio de la Santísima Trinidad Bolívar y Palacios Ponte y Blanco, better known as Simón Bolívar, is also known as the "George Washington of South America." He led Bolivia, Colombia, Ecuador, Panama, Peru, and Venezuela to independence from Spanish rule.

THE RIGHT STUFF

Chuck Yeager, the first person to break the sound barrier in a plane, is the uncle of former MLB catcher Steve Yeager, who played fourteen seasons with the Los Angeles Dodgers.

When Chuck was a young boy, his older brother, Roy, accidentally killed his infant sister, Doris Ann, with a shotgun.

Yeager had keen 20/10 vision when he enlisted in the U.S. Army Air Forces just before America entered World War II.

Yeager's P-51 Mustang fighter was shot down on his eighth mission over France, and he managed to make his way to Spain over the Pyrenees.

Yeager later became "ace in a day" when he shot down five enemy planes in one mission.

ONE SMALL STEP

Neil Armstrong, the first person to set foot on the moon, was also command pilot on the *Gemini 8* mission and was the first person to dock two spacecraft.

Armstrong only spent two and a half hours outside on the lunar surface.

Armstrong once threatened to sue his barber for selling his hair clippings without permission.

Armstrong stopped signing autographs in 1994.

UNKNIGHTED

In 1923, Benito Mussolini was granted an honorary knighthood by the British Crown. It was annulled in 1940.

GETTING TO KNOW YOU

Diana Spencer only met Prince Charles thirteen times before they were wed.

HAVE YOU BEEN A GOOD LITTLE THIEF?

St. Nicholas, the model for Santa Claus, is the patron saint of children, sailors, archers, and thieves.

MAKEUP MAVEN

Helena Rubinstein was born Chaja Rubenstein in Kraków, Poland.

Rubinstein began her beauty/cosmetics business in Australia, where she used the plentiful supply of lanolin from that country's sheep industry as the base for her beauty creams.

Rubinstein stood four feet, ten inches tall.

In 1940, Rubinstein was denied permission to take an apartment in a New York City building because she was Jewish, so she just bought the whole building instead.

One of Rubenstein's favorite lines was "There are no ugly women, only lazy ones."

DAYS OF YORE

TSAR POWER

Bulgaria, Russia, and Serbia all had tsars.

The first person to call himself "tsar" was Simeon I of Bulgaria in the tenth century.

The last tsar was Simeon Borisov, tsar of Bulgaria from 1943 until he was overthrown in 1946. Amazingly, he was elected prime minister of Bulgaria fifty-five years later, in 2001.

PAPAL POWER

Up until 533, popes kept their baptismal names. In that year, Mercurius took the name Pope John II because his given name was that of a Roman god.

Since the end of the tenth century, popes have generally chosen new names for themselves, but as late as 1555, some still kept their given names.

A pope can choose any name he wishes and usually does so to honor another, even a family member.

There has never been a Pope Peter II, because Peter is so revered that only he should have that honor.

Pope Benedict IX was pope three times between 1032 and 1048, being the only pope to hold the position more than once. After his second stint, he sold the papacy to Pope Gregory VI.

Pope Paul I, who held that title from 757 to 767, succeeded his brother, Pope Stephen II.

The only Englishman to ever be elected pope was Nicholas Breakspear, who served from 1154 to 1159, as Pope Adrian IV.

VERY EMPRESSIVE

The only woman to ever rule China was Empress Wu Zetian, whose dynasty lasted from 690 to 705.

BROKEN BELL

The Liberty Bell was commissioned by the Pennsylvania Assembly in 1751 to commemorate the fiftieth anniversary of William Penn's 1701 Charter of Privileges, Pennsylvania's original constitution.

The Liberty Bell was cast in England in 1752.

"Pennsylvania" is spelled "Pensylvania" on the bell, since that was the accepted spelling at the time.

The bell did not become iconic until it was used on the cover of an 1837 edition of *Liberty*, a publication of the New York Anti-Slavery Society. In fact, it was they who gave it the name "Liberty Bell." Before that, it was known as the "State House Bell."

The bell cracked the first time it was rung, in 1753, and was melted down and recast with a higher copper content to make it less brittle. This made the tone of the bell unacceptable and it was broken up and cast again.

The bell is composed of 70 percent copper, 25 percent tin, and small amounts of antimony, arsenic, gold, lead, nickel, silver, and zinc.

The strike note of the bell is E-flat.

In 1761, the bell tolled to honor King George III ascending the throne.

In 1777, the bell was removed and hidden in Allentown, Pennsylvania, to keep the British from melting it down to make cannons.

The bell did *not* ring on July 4, 1776.

Sometime in the early nineteenth century the bell acquired its large zigzag crack.

CHEW ON THIS

Chewing tobacco was the prevalent form of tobacco used in the United States, prior to being surpassed by cigarette smoking in the early twentieth century.

Spittoons were a common feature of most public places from the late 1800s to the 1930s.

Spittoons are still present in the United States Senate, and each Supreme Court justice has one next to his or her seat in the courtroom.

WHOLE LOTTA SHAKIN' GOIN' ON

On one day in 1977, Atlantic City mayor Joseph Lazarow shook more than 11,000 hands to break the old record for most handshakes in one day, 8,513, held by Teddy Roosevelt.

The Guinness record for longest single handshake is fifteen hours, thirty minutes, and forty-five seconds.

President George Washington bowed instead of shaking hands, which he thought to be too "common" for his office.

HE SAILED THE OCEAN BLUE

Christopher Columbus's name in Italian is Cristoforo Colombo.

Columbus took seventeen ships on his second voyage to the New World.

Columbus demanded that the Spanish Crown pay him 10 percent of all their profits made in the New World as he was guaranteed in a contract he signed with them. The Crown reneged and Columbus and his estate sued.

Columbus was first buried in Spain. His remains were then moved to Santo Domingo (Dominican Republic); Havana, Cuba; and then back to Spain.

WORMHOLES

Most earthworms are not native to North America and were probably introduced by early European settlers.

SIOUX ME

A Lakota Sioux woman could divorce her husband at any time by simply moving in with relatives or another man, or putting all her husband's possessions outside their lodge.

Comanche men were polygamous, but an adulterous wife could be killed or have her nose cut off.

TEATIME

There was a second, "mini" Boston Tea Party, in 1774, where 16 chests of tea were thrown into Boston Harbor. During the more famous 1773 Tea Party, 342 chests were dumped.

HERE TODAY, GONE TOMORROW

Many once great civilizations suddenly disappeared from history for no known reason. Some notable examples include:

The Clovis, first inhabitants of the New World

The Olmec of Mexico

The Minoans of Crete

The Anasazi of the American Southwest

The Khmer of Cambodia

The Mycenaeans of Greece

PASSPORT PLEASE

One of the earliest forms of passport was a *bara'a* issued in the medieval Muslim world that showed the holder had paid his taxes. Without this receipt, one could not travel outside one's homeland.

The word "passport" comes from the practice of having to show a document to travel through the gate, or *porte*, of a city.

FOOTSTOOL EMPIRE

The Ottoman Empire existed from 1299 to 1923.

The use of the word "ottoman" for a footstool dates to 1806, when these tall, cylindrical footstools that resembled the tall, round hats of Ottoman officials came into fashion in Europe.

Sultan Selim I, ruler of the Ottoman Empire from 1512 to 1520, practiced fratricide, having his brothers and nephews killed when he ascended to the throne, to prevent them from taking power.

One seventeenth-century sultan of the Ottoman Empire had more than 150 women belonging to the harems of his two predecessors drowned in the Bosphorus.

THE GANG THAT COULDN'T SHOOT STRAIGHT

On June 28, 1914, six different assassins waited on the streets of Sarajevo along the motorcade route of Archduke Franz Ferdinand of Austria. The first two assassins did nothing as the convertible carrying Ferdinand passed by. The third assassin threw a bomb at the car that bounced off and blew up the car behind. The next two assassins did nothing as the motorcade sped by them. The sixth assassin, Gavrilo Princip, gave up on the plot and went to a deli. A little later, the archduke decided to visit the wounded in the hospital. As luck would have it, the driver took a wrong turn, which placed the car directly in front of Princip as he emerged from the deli. The driver stalled out the car trying to reverse, but Princip stepped forward and shot Ferdinand and his wife to death at point-blank range.

DELAYED DECLARATION

Worcester, Massachusetts, was the first Colonial American entity to declare its independence from Britain, on October 4, 1774. After that, another ninety or so local jurisdictions and colonies did likewise, before the Continental Congress approved the Declaration of Independence.

Only twelve of the original colonies voted for independence from Britain on July 2, 1776. New York needed until July 19 to cast its vote.

JUSTICE FOR ALL

Patriot John Adams defended the British soldiers involved in the killing of Americans at the Boston Massacre. He got the captain acquitted and saved two soldiers from the death penalty.

STATE OF FREEDOM

Maine was admitted to the Union as a free state in 1820 to counterbalance the admission of Missouri as a slave state.

SEDITIOUS SUSAN

Susan B. Anthony cast a ballot for Ulysses S. Grant in Rochester, New York, on November 5, 1872. She was arrested and convicted of the "crime" of voting. The U.S. district attorney's case stated that Anthony had voted, "at which time she was a woman."

MADE IN THE SHADES

In the mid-1800s, some believed color-tinted glasses were good for certain ailments.

Yellow- and brown-tinted lenses were prescribed for people with syphilis because sensitivity to light is one of the disease's symptoms. Pink glasses were worn to treat depression and blue-colored for insanity.

In the early 1900s, sunglasses were known as "sun cheaters" in America. "Cheaters" was a term for eyeglasses at the time.

Polarized sunglasses hit the market in 1936.

BETTER LATE THAN NEVER

It took Great Britain until 2006 to pay off its post–World War II Marshall Plan reconstruction aid debt of $4.5 billion to the United States.

OLD TECH

When IBM manufactured the first computer in 1954, their marketing department predicted sales of just six machines.

Walmart stopped selling VHS cassettes in 2006.

One hundred years ago, electric cars outsold gas-powered cars.

The first mass use of revolving doors was by the Piggly Wiggly market chain in the 1920s.

The zipper was originally used to close boots and tobacco pouches.

MONEYMAN

The British monetary system of pounds, shillings, and pence, which was used until 1971, was created by Charlemagne in the eighth century.

WANDERING JEWS

In 1290, King Edward I expelled all the Jews from England. Many ended up in Poland. They were not officially allowed back in the country until 1656.

WITH THIS RING . . .

During the 1800s, silver and gold thimbles were given by the groom to his bride-to-be at the time of their engagement. The top of the thimble could be cut off and worn as a ring after the wedding.

LADIES' CHOICE

A derringer pistol was used to kill Abraham Lincoln. The gun is very small and was a favorite of ladies years ago, prompting it to be known as a "muff gun" back in the day.

HISTORICAL BRIEFS

The Atlantic Ocean was known as the Western Ocean in the American colonies.

The Vikings ventured as far south as the Middle East.

From 1838 to 1902, it was against the law to swim during daylight hours in Australia. Doing so was considered immoral. One could only swim before dawn and after dusk and never with members of the opposite sex.

The "RMS" in RMS *Titanic* stands for Royal Mail Ship. The boat carried British mail as well as passengers.

BATTLE ZONE

WEIRD WEAPONS

Japan launched nine thousand incendiary balloons into the jet stream during World War II, three hundred of which landed on their target, the U.S. mainland. They came down all across the western United States, from California to Texas to Detroit. None, however, hit any target of value.

The U.S. Navy tested cat bombs during World War II. The idea was to put a cat inside a bomb that the cat could steer and drop near an enemy ship at sea. The thinking was that since cats are afraid of water, they would steer the bomb to a ship. The plan had two simple flaws—cats aren't afraid of water and the g-forces from being dropped from a plane caused the kitties to pass out.

An American dentist came up with a unique plan to burn down Tokyo, which was actually approved by FDR. One million bats with napalm strapped to them were to be dropped from airplanes over the city. When the bats went to roost on Tokyo's mainly wooden structures, a great conflagration would occur. The plan probably would have worked, but the bats managed to get loose at the U.S. air base in Carlsbad, New Mexico, and burned it to the ground instead.

Another highly original weapon design involving animals was the Pigeon Project, where pigeons were trained to guide missiles at ships by pecking on the image of the ship projected on a screen in the nose of the missile. The plan worked in testing, but the navy wasn't comfortable having birds guide their weapons.

During World War II, the Soviet Union developed a flying tank. Known as the A40 Tank Wing, it was designed to be dropped from under an airplane and glide to the ground. It actually managed to glide and land smoothly on its test flight, but proved too heavy for Soviet airplanes to carry effectively.

Also during World War II, the Soviet Army trained explosive-laden dogs to run under German tanks, where they were detonated. The U.S. military also trained "anti-tank" dogs, in 1943, but never used them. The Soviet Union continued training these "anti-tank" dogs until 1996.

More recently, Iran attempted to train "kamikaze" dolphins to seek out and blow up submarines.

The U.S. Navy has developed a laser powerful enough to burn through twenty feet of steel in a second.

The U.S. Department of Defense has tested an unmanned plane that has reached Mach 20, or about thirteen thousand miles per hour. The Falcon Hypersonic Technology Vehicle (HTV) is launched from a rocket and comes back to Earth with such speed that it heats up to 3,500°F. The military's ultimate goal is to use the plane to be able to strike an enemy target anywhere in the world in an hour's time.

ISLAND INVASION

The United States attacked Puerto Rico in 1898, during the Spanish-American War. Spain ceded the island to the United States after their defeat.

TOP GUNS

The catapult on a U.S. aircraft carrier can launch a plane from 0 to 120 miles per hour in just three seconds.

The arrester cables on an aircraft carrier have to be replaced after every 125 landings.

Aircraft carriers carry about 2.4 million gallons of jet fuel and have to be refilled every few days.

A combat jet can use up to twenty gallons of fuel in a minute.

FUSSY FIGHTERS

The U.S. military's F-22 Raptor fighter jet cost $412 million per plane to build. There are 158 of them.

It takes about three thousand people to maintain each Raptor.

For every one hour of flight time, the plane requires forty-five hours of maintenance.

The Raptor, which debuted in 2005, has never been used in combat.

A HOUSE DIVIDED

The distance from Washington, DC (capital of the Union during the Civil War), to Richmond, Virginia (capital of the Confederacy), is only 107 miles.

During the Civil War, Washington, DC, was the most fortified city in the world.

The Battle of Shiloh is also known as the Battle of Pittsburg Landing. It was the bloodiest battle in American history up until that time. "Shiloh" is a Hebrew word meaning "place of peace."

The youngest soldier in the Civil War was eight-year-old Avery Brown, who lied and said he was twelve so that he could become the drummer boy for Company C, Thirty-first Ohio Volunteer Infantry.

One hundred thousand Union soldiers were under the age of fifteen.

Southerners who owned twenty or more slaves did not have to fight in the Civil War.

The Union's ironclad ship—the *Monitor*—was the first warship to have flush toilets.

Although Kentucky proper did not secede from the Union, part of the state was occupied by Confederate troops and those counties were admitted to the Confederacy.

George Armstrong Custer was promoted from the rank of captain to brigadier general three days before the Battle of Gettysburg, at age twenty-three, making him one of the youngest generals in U.S. military history.

Custer's cavalry brigade lost more men at the Battle of Gettysburg than any other Union cavalry brigade—257.

The largest artillery barrage in the history of the Western Hemisphere occurred at the Battle of Gettysburg.

In 1864, the Confederate submarine *H.L. Hunley* became the world's first sub to sink an enemy ship in combat. The sub then mysteriously sank to the bottom of the ocean off the coast of Charleston, South Carolina.

"Dixie" was a blackface minstrel song written by a Northerner in the 1850s. It tells the story of a freed slave wishing he were back on the plantation.

General Ulysses S. Grant hated rare meat and the sight of blood.

At the outset of the Civil War, Grant wasn't even in the army. He was working at his father's dry goods store.

> Private John J. Williams of the Thirty-fourth Indiana was the last man killed in the final battle of the Civil War at Palmito Ranch, Texas, on May 13, 1865, a rebel victory.

Union general Daniel Sickles lost his leg at the Battle of Gettysburg in 1863. He had the amputated bones donated to the Army Medical Museum in Washington, DC, and visited them repeatedly for the next fifty years. The bones are still on display today, at the National Museum of Health and Medicine in Silver Springs, Maryland.

> Confederate lieutenant general Nathan Bedford Forrest began the war as a private and ended up a division commander.

Forrest is believed to have had thirty horses shot out from under him during the war and personally killed thirty-one men in close combat. He later quipped, "I was a horse ahead at the end."

> Forrest became the first grand wizard of the Ku Klux Klan after the war.

The greatest financial asset of the United States before the Civil War was its slave population.

> Before the Civil War, the job of nursing wounded soldiers was a male occupation.

The last Civil War veteran died in 1959.

WORLD AT WAR

During World War II, Nazi minister of the interior Heinrich Himmler was so worried about German troops contracting sexual diseases from French prostitutes that he hatched a plan, approved by Hitler, to supply the soldiers with blow-up Aryan sex dolls. The "Borghild Project," as it was known, created about fifty blond-haired, blue-eyed dolls called "gynoids." The idea died a quiet death when it was rejected by the men, who preferred the real thing.

The weather was so cold during the Battle of the Bulge, in January 1945, that weapons often froze and soldiers had to urinate on them to thaw them out.

The only part of Britain that was occupied by the Germans during World War II was the Channel Islands.

There are still approximately 20 million land mines from World War II scattered around Egypt. Britain, Germany, and Italy have given funds to help remove them.

One of Adolf Hitler's nephews—William Patrick Hitler—escaped Germany and enlisted in the U.S. Navy in 1944. After the war, he changed his last name to Stuart-Houston.

During World War II, the Soviet Union trained one thousand female pilots and had three all-women aviation regiments, one known as the "Night Witches," a night bomber regiment.

One female Soviet pilot—Lydia Litvyak—shot down twelve German planes during World War II. She is one of only two female fighter aces ever in the world, the other being Soviet Yekaterina Budanova, who had eleven kills.

Twelve thousand Allied bombers were shot down over Europe and one hundred thousand aviators were killed during World War II.

Two months after the Germans surrendered in World War II, British prime minister Winston Churchill was voted out of office.

Kazuo Sakamaki became the first Japanese prisoner of war when the midget sub he was in during the attack on Pearl Harbor became disabled and he was captured.

In 1941, Josef Stalin issued Order 270 that prohibited any Soviet soldier from surrendering, even if totally encircled by the Germans, which often happened. Violators were to be shot and their families arrested or denied any state aid.

In 1942, Stalin issued Order 227, which prohibited Soviet units from retreating without an order. It also created "penal" companies that were comprised of soldiers with disciplinary problems. These units were assigned to the most dangerous areas of the front lines. "Blocking" companies were deployed at the rear of the fighting, with orders to shoot anyone caught trying to withdraw or desert.

It is claimed that during World War I, a German submarine sank a British merchant ship only to be sunk herself by a truck hurled into the sub from the exploding ship.

In World War II, a German U-boat was disabled when the RAF Wellington bomber it had shot out of the sky crashed into its side. Other RAF planes then sank the sub.

In U.S. military parlance, only submarines are referred to as "boats." Surface vessels are "ships."

Nagasaki was not the primary target the day the United States dropped the atomic bomb on that city. Kokura was the first choice, but cloud cover over that metropolis forced the bomber to its secondary target— Nagasaki.

Many American POWs were killed when Nagasaki was bombed.

The Nagasaki blast created winds with speeds up to 624 miles per hour.

The bomb dropped on Nagasaki was called Fat Man after the character, Kasper Gutman, played by Sydney Greenstreet in *The Maltese Falcon*, who was short and fat, like the bomb.

YO HO HO

Rum was a part of the British Navy's daily rations until 1970.

GIVE PEACE A CHANCE

The Three Hundred and Thirty-Five Years' War between the Netherlands and the Isles of Scilly (part of the United Kingdom off the coast of Cornwall) is the longest "war" in history. There were no casualties, but the two belligerents were technically at war from 1651 until peace was finally declared in 1986.

HOLD ON HOLDOUT

The longest siege in military history was the Ottoman siege of the Venetian-ruled city of Candia, Crete, which lasted twenty-one years, from 1648 until 1669.

DAVY JONES'S LOCKER

During the First Punic War between Rome and the Carthaginians in 255 BC, a Roman fleet was destroyed by a storm off the coast of Sicily, killing more than ninety thousand men, nearly 15 percent of Italy's adult male population.

The greatest number of vessels ever involved in a naval battle was probably in the Japanese Battle of Dan-no-ura, in 1185, where eight hundred ships from the Minamoto clan defeated the five hundred ships of the Taira clan.

DECREPIT DOGE

The oldest military commander was Venetian Doge Enrico Dandolo, who was ninety-seven and blind when he directed the sacking of Constantinople during the fourth Crusade in 1204.

DISARMED AND DE-FINGERED

In the 1500s, the French would cut off the fingers of English longbowmen they captured, to prevent them from using a bow in the future.

The last person killed in combat by a longbow was an unfortunate German soldier shot by English captain John Churchill during the English retreat to Dunkirk in 1940.

BOMBS AWAY

The first known military assault from the air was in 1849 when a bomb was dropped from an Austrian hot air balloon in Italy.

FEATHERED FOES

Back in the day, carrier pigeons were used for military communications, and falcons were trained to intercept these feathered messengers.

PAPER TIGERS

For hundreds of years, Chinese warriors wore armor made of pleated paper.

FEEL THE HEAT

The Tsar hydrogen bomb detonated by the Soviet Union in 1961 is the most powerful man-made explosion ever. It had a force of fifty megatons, or more than 50 million tons of TNT.

> The Tsar bomb had ten times the power of all the explosives used in World War II, but only one-quarter the estimated power of the volcanic eruption of Krakatau in 1883.

The mushroom cloud the bomb generated went straight up forty miles, and the blast destroyed buildings seventy miles away.

> The bomb's inventor, Andrei Sakharov, later became an antinuclear activist and won the Nobel Peace Prize in 1975. The Soviets didn't allow him to attend the ceremony in Stockholm.

THE PRICE OF VICTORY

Hellfire missiles that are fired from aerial drones cost about $58,000 each.

> Tomahawk cruise missiles go for $600,000 a pop.

BOUNCING BALLS

At the beginning of the American Revolution, Fort Sullivan was built on an island in the harbor at Charleston, South Carolina. The fort was made out of palmetto logs.

These logs were rather soft and spongy, so that when the British attacked the fort in June 1776, their cannonballs bounced right off. The British fleet was beaten back, for what is claimed to be the first American victory of the war.

DUBIOUS DISTINCTION

Charles Lindbergh received the Commander Cross of the Order of the German Eagle in 1938 from high-ranking Nazi official Hermann Göring.

STAY-AT-HOME GENERAL

During his time in command of the war in Korea, General Douglas MacArthur never spent a night there, preferring to return to his digs in Japan.

TIMBER!

It took six thousand mature oak trees to build one large warship in the early 1800s.

SPEAKING OF . . .

MANY TONGUES

There are about seven thousand languages spoken on Earth.

Hundreds of languages have fewer than fifty speakers.

Languages are disappearing at a rate of about two a month.

GOING, GOING . . .

There are only two remaining speakers, in southern Mexico, of Ayapanec, a language that is thought to have descended from the pre-Columbian Olmec culture that once thrived in Mexico.

Not far away from the aforementioned last two speakers of Ayapanec live a handful of people who still speak a dialect of Nahuatl, the language of the Aztecs.

NATIVE AMERICAN

In the United States, Oklahoma has the highest density of indigenous languages, mostly because of the forced relocation of Native American tribes to that area in the 1800s.

Along the coast of the Carolinas and Georgia live 250,000 people of the Gullah-Geechee culture. They are descendants of African slaves who worked on rice plantations.

The Gullah have their own language, which is a mix of English, Creole, and African dialects.

American soldiers used Gullah during World War II as a code language.

Tagalog is a language spoken by 1.5 million people in the United States. It is an Austronesian language that is primarily spoken in the Philippines.

SEPARATED BY A COMMON LANGUAGE

Modern Standard Arabic is the proper, formal written Arabic derived from the Koran, but few speak it at home. There are numerous dialects across the Arab world, and people from one region may not be able to understand those from another region.

COLOR BLIND

Many languages in Asia and Africa have no word distinguishing blue from green. Traditional Japanese is one example. While modern Japanese has a word for "green,"

green traffic lights and leaves are still referred to as "blue," a throwback to earlier usage.

Many African languages do not distinguish blue from black, while other languages treat light blue and dark blue as separate colors, unlike English.

YOU DON'T SAY

The Kikuyu tribe of Kenya used to consider the number ten so unlucky that they wouldn't speak the word. Instead they said "full nine."

MEN OF FEW WORDS

Taki Taki, or Sranan, a language spoken in Suriname, has the fewest words of any language—340.

NAMESAKES

The word "boycott" was coined after nineteenth-century English landlord Charles C. Boycott, an English land agent in Ireland in 1880 who was ostracized by the local community in a fight over tenants' rights. His neighbors wouldn't talk to him, workers refused to harvest his crops, stores and pubs wouldn't serve him, and the postmen refused to deliver his mail. Boycott's name has since become synonymous with organized isolation.

The word "derby" comes from one Edward Stanley, Twelfth Earl of Derby, who founded the Derby horse race in 1780, to which the hats were worn.

The word "draconian" is from the statesman Draco, who codified the laws in Athens in 621 BC.

The word "derrick" is named for seventeenth-century English hangman Thomas Derrick, whose gallows used a system of cables and pulleys.

The word "shrapnel" is from English artilleryman Henry Shrapnel, who invented a shell with lead balls to cause as many casualties as possible.

The word "silhouette" comes from eighteenth-century French finance minister Etienne de Silhouette.

The Zamboni used to resurface ice rinks is named for its American inventor Frank Zamboni, who owned a skating rink.

Earl Grey tea is named after Charles Grey, Second Earl Grey, who was Britain's prime minister from 1830 to 1834. He supposedly once received a box of tea flavored with bergamot oil, a citrus fruit.

DEFINITIVE DATA

The word "democracy," comes from the Greek words *dêmos*, which means "people," and *kratos*, which means "power."

Those crossing city streets illegally became known as "jaywalkers" in the early twentieth century. At the time, the word "jay" referred to a country dweller who was stupid or foolish.

The expression "sold down the river" came from the slave markets in Virginia, where purchased slaves were then resold by middlemen to the cotton plantation owners down the Mississippi River.

Second-century Roman medical man Quintus Sammonicus Serenus is the first known person to use the word "abracadabra." He believed wearing an amulet with the word inscribed on it could ward off malaria.

In the Roman calendar, the ides were the fifteenth day of March, May, July, and October, and the thirteenth day of the other months. "Ides" comes from Latin, meaning "half month."

Heroin was once a registered trademark of Bayer. They marketed it as an over-the-counter drug beginning in 1895.

CLOCKWISE

Longcase clocks under five feet tall are known as "granddaughters," those over five feet are "grandmothers," and those over six feet tall are called "grandfather" clocks.

The term "grandfather clock" comes from an 1876 song titled "My Grandfather's Clock," about a longcase clock in an English hotel that stopped working on the day the old man who wound it died.

"Q"UITE USELESS WORDS

A "quoin" is a solid exterior angle, such as on a building.

"Quotidian" means "occurring every day."

A "quiff" is a prominent forelock.

A "quire" is a collection of twenty-four or twenty-five sheets of paper—one-twentieth of a ream.

A "quirt" is a short riding whip.

"Zaftig" means "pleasingly plump."

A "zerk" is a grease fitting.

"Zeroth" is being numbered zero in a series of numbers.

A "zetabyte" is one sextillion (1 with twenty-one zeros) bytes.

"Zeugma" is defined by Webster's as "the use of a word to modify or govern two or more words usually in such a manner that it applies to each in a different sense or makes sense with only one (as in 'opened the door and her heart to the homeless boy')."

"Zoonosis" is a disease that is communicable from animals to humans.

"Zydeco" is a musical genre of southern Louisiana incorporating elements of French, Caribbean, and blues music that features guitars, accordions, and washboards.

"Zygodactyl" is having the toes arranged two in front and two in back, as in some birds.

"Zygosity" is the characteristics of a zygote.

NAME THAT COMPANY

A&M Records was named after founders Herb Alpert and Jerry Moss.

A&W Root Beer was named for founders Roy Allen and Frank Wright.

Adobe Systems was named after the Adobe Creek in Santa Clara, California, which flowed behind the home of the company's cofounder.

Alcoa is short for Aluminum Company of America.

Amazon.com, which was originally called Cadabra.com, got its name from the river that has the highest volume, in hopes that the online company would have a higher sales volume than a traditional store.

AOL began as Quantum Computer Services.

Bayer was named for Friedrich Bayer, who started the company in 1863.

Black & Decker was named for founders S. Duncan Black and Alonzo Decker.

BMW is short for Bavaria Motor Works.

Bridgestone was named after founder Shojiro Ishibashi, whose last name means "bridge of stone."

Cisco Systems is short for San Francisco Systems.

CVS was originally Consumer Value Stores.

Dick's Sporting Goods was named for founder Dick Stack, who started a small tackle shop in 1948.

Duane Reade was named for the intersection of Duane and Reade streets in Manhattan where the first store was opened.

eBay began as AuctionWeb in 1995. The company founder wanted to register the domain name Echo Bay, but it was already taken by a gold mining company, so he shortened it to eBay.

Equifax is a combination of the words "equitable" and "factual."

Exxon is a made-up name derived from the company's regional name, Esso, in 1972. At first they considered the name "Exon," but the governor of Nebraska at the time had that last name, so they added the extra "x."

Ferrari was named for Enzo Ferrari.

Five Guys hamburger chain was named for founder Jerry Murrell and his four sons. Another son was born after the hamburger chain was founded and today the five sons are considered the "Five Guys."

Harpo Productions comes from Oprah spelled backward.

Hasbro derives from a contraction of its founders' names, the Hassenfeld brothers.

HP, Hewlett-Packard, would have been Packard-Hewlett if Dave Packard had won a coin toss with Bill Hewlett over whose name should go first.

Hitachi means "sunrise" in Japanese.

Intel was going to be called Integrated Electronics, but the name was already taken, so it was shortened to Intel.

Lancôme was inspired by the founder's trip to Le Château de Lancôme, a French castle, in 1935.

Lukoil comes from the first letter of the three Russian companies that merged to create this oil giant—Langepasneftagaz, Uraineftegaz, and Kogalymneftegaz.

Lycos derives from Lycosidae, the family name of wolf spiders.

Mitsubishi means "three diamonds" in Japanese. (The company used to make zero fighter planes during World War II and the three-diamond logo represents a stylized airplane propeller.)

Motorola used to make car radios. The company name was adopted in 1930 as a contraction of "motor" and "Victrola," an early phonograph sold by RCA.

Nabisco used to be National Biscuit Company.

Nestlé, which means "little nest" in Swabian German, was founded by Henri Nestlé.

Nike was named for the Greek goddess of victory.

Nokia began as a wood-pulp mill in Nokia, Finland.

Pepsi was named for pepsin, a digestive enzyme used in the cola's original recipe.

Procter & Gamble was founded by candle maker William Procter and soap maker James Gamble in 1837. They met after marrying two sisters.

Qantas stands for Queensland and Northern Territory Aerial Services.

QVC stands for quality, value, and convenience.

Samsung means "three stars" in Korean.

Sanyo means "three oceans" in Japanese.

Sega is short for Service Games, founded by American Marty Bromley to import pinball machines to American military bases in Japan.

Sharp Electronics' first product was an ever-sharp pencil.

Shell Oil Company has its roots in a company that imported Japanese seashells.

Skype was originally going to be called Sky-Peer-to-Peer.

Sony is from the Latin word *sonus*, meaning "sound."

Sprint was named after its former parent company, Southern Pacific Railroad International. In the old days, communication lines were laid alongside railways since the paths were already cleared.

TCBY was originally known as "This Can't Be Yogurt" but was forced to change to "The Country's Best Yogurt" after being sued by a competitor with a similar name.

Verizon derives from the Latin word for "truth," *veritas*, and the word "horizon."

Volvo is from the Latin word *volvo*, meaning "I roll." It was originally the name of a ball bearing.

> Wachovia is the Latinized version of the Austrian name "Wachau," a region of North Carolina near Winston-Salem, the company's birthplace.

Williams-Sonoma was founded by Chuck Williams in Sonoma, California.

> Yahoo! got its name from the Jonathan Swift book *Gulliver's Travels*, in which a "yahoo" is someone who is repulsively unattractive, rude, and uncouth. (Some have suggested that Yahoo! really stands for "Yet Another Hierarchical Officious Oracle.")

HORSEPOWER

The Mitsubishi Eclipse is named for an eighteenth-century English racehorse.

CODE WORDS

In Morse code, SOS is a sequence of three dots / three dashes / three dots, all run together.

> SOS does not stand for anything, for example, "Save our ships," but was chosen as a distress signal because it is easily transmitted.

The "@" symbol was added to the Morse code alphabet in 2011, the first addition in the last seventy years.

NOTEWORTHY

Musical notation was invented in the early eleventh century by Italian monk Guido of Arezzo. He used *ut* (since replaced with *do*), *re*, *mi*, *fa*, *sol*, and *la* to name the first six tones of the major scale.

SPORTING NEWS

PITCHMAN

Babe Ruth pitched all fourteen innings of Game 2 of the 1916 World Series, for the Boston Red Sox against the Brooklyn Robins, which is still the record for a complete game in World Series history. The Red Sox won 2–1.

That same year, Ruth compiled a record of 23–12 and led the league in earned run average (1.75) and shutouts (nine). Between 1915 and 1918 he had a 78–40 record.

BATTER UP

Ichiro Suzuki holds the MLB record for most consecutive 200-hit seasons, with ten. He is followed by Wee Willie Keeler with eight, Wade Boggs with seven, and Chuck Klein with five.

"SHATTERING" THE RECORD

In the first three months of the 2008 MLB season, a record 750 bats were shattered. This was a result of the majors switching from ash to maple bats. The bats that broke were found to have the grain running on an angle near the handle, instead of straight up. To make the direction of the wood's grain obvious, Major League Baseball mandated that bat manufacturers put a black ink spot on the handles that bleeds along the grain. This allows inspectors to see the angle of the grain and ensure that fibers run at an angle of no more than three degrees from vertical.

MILLION-DOLLAR MEN

New York Yankees third baseman Alex Rodriguez made $32 million in salary for the 2011 season, just $4.1 million less than the entire payroll of the Kansas City Royals.

In 2011, the Yankees had the top four highest-paid players in Major League Baseball.

THE 3,000

Twenty-eight Major League Baseball players have collected at least three thousand hits in their careers.

Fourteen of these players batted right-handed, twelve left-handed, and two were switch-hitters.

The Cleveland Indians had three different players reach three thousand hits while on their roster—Nap Lajoie, Tris Speaker, and Eddie Murray.

Derek Jeter is the only New York Yankee to ever accumulate three thousand hits. Dave Winfield and Rickey Henderson did so, but they played for several teams. Jeter has spent his entire career with the Yanks.

Jeter was the seventh-fastest player to reach the three-thousand-hit mark. Ty Cobb, Nap Lajoie, Tony Gwynn, Stan Musial, Honus Wagner, and Tris Speaker did so in fewer games.

Babe Ruth, Lou Gehrig, Joe DiMaggio, and Mickey Mantle never got three thousand hits.

Four players have three thousand hits and five hundred home runs—Hank Aaron, Willie Mays, Eddie Murray, and Rafael Palmeiro.

Roberto Clemente had exactly three thousand hits. He hit the three thousandth on the last at bat of his career, before he died in a plane crash.

SLAMMIN' SAMMY

Samuel Peralta "Sammy" Sosa, who is from the Dominican Republic, holds the record for most home runs hit by a foreign-born major-league player—609.

Sosa also is the only MLB player to hit sixty or more home runs in three different seasons.

Sosa was caught using a "corked" bat in 2003 and also failed a test for performance-enhancing drugs in that year.

In 2009, Sosa admitted using a cream to lighten his skin.

BEST LOSERS

In 1910, pitcher Ed Walsh of the Chicago White Sox had an ERA of 1.27 and yet lost twenty games. He also holds the all-time record for lowest career ERA—1.82.

Hall of Famers Cy Young and Walter Johnson both lost twenty games in a season.

FOLLOW THE BOUNCING BALL

Before 1930, baseballs that bounced over the outfield wall were home runs. They are now ground rule doubles.

SUCCESSFUL SWINGERS

The University of Southern California baseball team has won the most College World Series—twelve. Louisiana State University and Texas have won six each, and Arizona State has won five.

CHEERS!

As of 2011, six NFL teams had no cheerleaders—the Chicago Bears, Cleveland Browns, Detroit Lions, Green Bay Packers, New York Giants, and Pittsburgh Steelers. The Browns, Lions, and Giants have never had cheerleaders in their histories.

The Packers sent their cheerleaders packing in 1988, after a survey showed their fans didn't care about having them at games.

The Baltimore Colts were the first NFL team to get cheerleaders, in 1954.

Most NFL cheerleaders perform for one to four years.

Some famous women that used to be NFL cheerleaders include:

Phyllis Smith, who plays Phyllis on *The Office*, cheered for the old St. Louis Cardinals.

Laurie Flynn, wife of quarterback Matt Schaub, was an Atlanta Falcons cheerleader.

Kollette Klassen, wife of quarterback Jake Plummer, cheered for the Denver Broncos.

Jeanette Dousdebes, wife of Marco Rubio, the U.S. senator for Florida, cheered for the Miami Dolphins.

Paige Green, wife of quarterback John Elway, cheered for the Raiders.

Jenilee Harrison, who played Cindy Snow on *Three's Company*, cheered for the Rams.

Apollonia Kotero, ex-girlfriend of Prince, cheered for the Rams.

Charisma Carpenter, who played Cordelia Chase on *Buffy the Vampire Slayer*, cheered for the Chargers.

Some of the NFL cheerleading squad names have included the Buffalo Jills, Carolina Topcats, Cincinnati Ben-Gals, New Orleans Saintsations, Jets Flight Crew, and Seattle Sea Gals.

THREE CHEERS FOR GRANDMA!

In 2011, the only NFL cheerleader to be a grandmother was thirty-seven-year-old Oakland Raiderette Susie Sanchez.

BEST OF THE BEST

Jack Nicklaus has won the most major professional golf championships—eighteen.

Patty Berg has won the most major women's professional golf championships—fifteen.

Roger Federer has won the most Grand Slam singles tennis titles—sixteen. He is ahead of Pete Sampras (fourteen), Roy Emerson (twelve), Björn Borg (eleven), and Rod Laver (eleven).

Jim Hoiser of Wayne, New Jersey, has recorded 112 perfect 300 games in his bowling career. Five others also have more than one hundred perfect scores.

Figure skater Michelle Kwan has won nine U.S. championships.

RUN FOR THE ROSES

Only eleven horses have won horse racing's Triple Crown.

In Triple Crown races, colts carry 126 pounds and fillies 121 pounds.

The fastest time ever clocked at the Kentucky Derby was one minute and fifty-nine and two-fifths seconds, set by Secretariat in 1973.

MR. CLUTCH

Ex–Los Angeles Laker Jerry West was known as "Mr. Clutch" for his knack for making big plays in big games, such as his buzzer-beating sixty-three-foot shot to tie Game 3 of the 1970 NBA Finals against the New York Knicks.

> West holds the record for highest point average during a playoff series—46.3.

West is the only player to win the NBA Finals MVP award who played for the losing team, in 1969.

> West played his entire career with the Lakers (1960–74) and went to fourteen all-star games.

HISTORIC HOOPS

The oldest conference in college basketball is the Big Ten, established in 1899.

> Basketball inventor James Naismith also founded the University of Kansas basketball program.

HARD TIMES

Former Chicago Bulls superstar Scottie Pippen lost most of his $110 million in NBA earnings through bad investments and was forced to hold a yard sale, where he sold his NBA memorabilia, artwork, and Beanie Babies.

JERSEY BOYS

The top-selling NBA jerseys during the 2010-11 season were those of LeBron James, Kobe Bryant, Rajon Rondo, Amar'e Stoudemire, and Derrick Rose.

GIVE ME FIVE

The "high five" originated among basketball players in the 1960s. (The "low five" is known to have existed since the late 1920s.)

THEY MIGHT BE GIANTS

In 1929, the New York Football Giants original owner Tim Mara bought the entire Detroit Wolverines team just to get one player—quarterback Benny Friedman.

> When the stock market crashed, Tim Mara lost his shirt and, because of pending lawsuits against him, transferred ownership of the team to his two sons—Jack, age twenty-two, and Wellington, age fourteen—making Wellington the youngest owner of a professional sports franchise.

Wellington Mara was named after the Duke of Wellington.

Giants lineman Cal Hubbard, who went on to become a Major League Baseball umpire, is the only man in both the Pro Football Hall of Fame and the National Baseball Hall of Fame.

The famous 1934 NFL Championship Game between the Giants and the Chicago Bears at New York's Polo Grounds is known as the "Sneakers Game" because the Giants changed from cleats to sneakers at halftime to get better traction on the icy field and beat the Bears, who continued to slip in their cleats. The Giants had no sneakers at the start of the game and all the stores were closed because it was Sunday, so they had an assistant borrow nine pairs from Manhattan College.

The first two names of legendary Giants quarterback Y. A. Tittle were Yelberton Abraham.

Tittle played three seasons with the Baltimore Colts and ten with the San Francisco 49ers before he was traded to the Giants in 1961.

Giants Pro Bowl end Homer Jones was the first NFL player to "spike" the ball, a term he coined, after his first touchdown of the 1965 season.

New York Giants Hall of Fame linebacker Lawrence Taylor maintained that when the team played road games, players from opposing teams would often send call girls to his hotel room to keep him up all night. He didn't mind.

OUR HOUSE

The Chicago Bears home stadium, Soldier Field, has the lowest seating capacity in the NFL at 61,500.

The Washington Redskins stadium, FedEx Field, has the most seats with 91,704.

A COLD SHOWER

Many sources credit the first postgame "Gatorade shower" to Jim Burt and Harry Carson of the New York Giants after their win over the Washington Redskins in 1985. Dan Hampton of the Chicago Bears claimed he invented it when he doused head coach Mike Ditka after a win over the Minnesota Vikings in 1984.

> Harry Carson went on to dump a Gatorade cooler full of popcorn over President Ronald Reagan during the team's trip to the White House to celebrate their Super Bowl win in 1987.

Coach George Allen of the Long Beach State football team may have died as a result of the ice water shower he received after a November 1990 win over the University of Nevada, Las Vegas. The seventy-two-year-old Allen reported being in ill health after the incident. He died six weeks later.

BY THE NUMBERS

The most frequently occurring NFL score is 20–17.

> There were 11,283 points scored in the 2010 NFL season.

Green Bay Packers quarterback Aaron Rodgers's number 12 jersey was the bestselling football jersey in 2011.

At the end of the 2010 season, the Chicago Bears had the most ever NFL wins with 721. The Green Bay Packers were number two with 693.

FAME, WHAT'S YOUR NAME?

Fifteen Pro Football Hall of Famers played for junior colleges.

USC has the most former football players who are in the Pro Football Hall of Fame—eleven. Notre Dame is second with ten, Michigan and Ohio State each have eight, and Alabama and Syracuse have seven each.

Some lesser-known colleges that produced future NFL Hall of Famers include Bethune-Cookman (Florida), Bishop College (Texas), Centenary College (Louisiana), Fort Valley State (Georgia), Geneva College (Pennsylvania), Hardin-Simmons University (Texas), University of Maryland-Eastern Shore, Milliken University (Illinois), Mississippi Vocational, New York University, North Carolina A&T, Northwestern Louisiana, Phillips University (Oklahoma), Prairie View A&M (Texas), Randolph Macon College (Virginia), Regis College (Massachusetts), Washington & Jefferson (Pennsylvania), and West Virginia Wesleyan.

The states that have produced the most Hall of Famers are Texas (twenty-eight), Pennsylvania (twenty-seven), Ohio (twenty-three), and Illinois (seventeen).

There are twenty-three quarterbacks in the NFL Hall of Fame and only three kickers.

Eight Heisman Trophy winners have made it into the Hall of Fame—Doak Walker, Paul Hornung, Roger Staubach, O. J. Simpson, Tony Dorsett, Earl Campbell, Marcus Allen, and Barry Sanders.

The players who received the highest ever vote percentage to get into the National Baseball Hall of Fame were Tom Seaver with 98.84 percent, Nolan Ryan with 98.79 percent, Cal Ripken Jr. with 98.53 percent, Ty Cobb with 98.23 percent, George Brett with 98.19 percent, and Hank Aaron with 97.83 percent.

Cy Young, the pitcher who won the most major-league games in history (511), only got 76 percent of the vote (fifth lowest ever) when he was inducted into the Hall of Fame in 1937. Other low-percentage vote getters include Al Simmons, Ferguson Jenkins, Willie Keeler, and Ralph Kiner with 75 percent and Early Wynn with 76 percent.

DIE-HARD FANS

In 2011, soccer enthusiasts brought the body of a dead seventeen-year-old fan to a professional match in Colombia.

In Turkey, soccer teams that have had too much violence in the stands ban men from all matches, only allowing women and children under twelve to attend.

A new study has found that when a sports fan's team wins a close game, that fan has a higher risk of dying in a car accident on the way home from the game.

Traffic deaths increase in the hometowns of winning professional sports teams, even if they played an away game.

Seventy percent of British soccer fans admit to having cried while at a match.

HAVES AND HAVE-NOTS

Two European soccer teams have the highest payrolls per player of any professional sports teams in the world. Barcelona's average player salary in the 2009–10 season was $7.9 million, while Real Madrid's was $7.4 million. The New York Yankees had the third-highest average payroll per player at $6.8 million. They were followed by the Los Angeles Lakers and the Orlando Magic of the NBA.

The minimum weekly salary in each of America's four top team sports leagues is $6,258 in the NFL; $7,972 in MLB; $9,108 in the NBA; and $9,615 in the NHL.

FOREIGN AFFAIRS

The British soccer teams Manchester United and Liverpool are owned by Americans.

HOT AND COLD

Romania has won 292 medals in the Summer Olympics, mainly for gymnastics, and just one in the Winter Games—a bronze in the 1968 two-man bobsled.

NO SHORTAGE OF TALENT

The shortest players in the four major American sports leagues in 2011 were:

> Major League Baseball: Tim Collins of the Kansas City Royals at five foot seven

> National Basketball Association: Earl Boykins of the Milwaukee Bucks at five foot five

> National Football League: Darren Sproles of the New Orleans Saints and Stefan Logan of the Detroit Lions at five foot six

> National Hockey League: Nathan Gerbe of the Buffalo Sabres at five foot five

HOP TO IT

Anthony Robles, a one-legged college wrestler, had a 36–0 record in 2011 and won the NCAA 125-pound national title.

GREATEST GRUNTER

Maria Sharapova holds the record for loudest grunt on the tennis court at 105 decibels.

HOME COURT DISADVANTAGE

No British male has won the Wimbledon title since Fred Perry did it back in 1936.

PARDON MY FRENCH

The French Open is more properly known as the Roland Garros Tournament in France, after the famous French aviator who was the first to fly across the Mediterranean.

RINGMASTERS

Puerto Rican boxer Wilfred Benitez is the youngest fighter to win a world boxing championship. He won the WBA light welterweight belt at age seventeen in 1976.

> Benitez made millions of dollars in his career, but ended up destitute, wheelchair-bound, and unable to speak due to numerous blows to the head during his career.

Ex–heavyweight boxing champ Larry Holmes left school for good in the seventh grade.

WEIGHING IN

The lightest weight class in professional boxing is minimum weight/mini flyweight, which has a limit of 105 pounds. The next heaviest class is light flyweight/jr. flyweight at 108 pounds; flyweight at 112 pounds; super flyweight/jr. bantamweight at 115 pounds; super bantamweight/jr. featherweight at 122 pounds; featherweight at 126 pounds; super featherweight/jr. lightweight at 130 pounds; lightweight at 135 pounds; super lightweight/jr. welterweight at 140 pounds; welterweight at 147 pounds; super welterweight/jr. middleweight at 154 pounds; middleweight at 160 pounds; super middleweight at 168 pounds;

light heavyweight at 175 pounds; cruiserweight at 200 pounds; and heavyweight, any weight above 200 pounds.

ROYAL EXEMPTION

Britain's Princess Anne was a member of the national equestrian team and the only participant in the 1976 Olympic Games who was not required to take a sex test first.

RACIAL REVIEW

For the 2011 Major League Baseball season, only 8.5 percent of the players were black, while more than 80 percent of NBA players were black and more than 60 percent in the NFL were.

Woody Strode and Kenny Washington were the first black players in the NFL during the modern era, having been signed by the Los Angeles Rams in 1946.

SPEED DEMONS

Richard Petty invented the netting that is placed over the open windows of NASCAR cars to prevent the driver's arms and head from coming out during a crash.

Richard Petty's father, Lee Petty, was the first person to crash in a Winston Cup race, wrecking on the 107th lap of a 1949 race in Charlotte, North Carolina.

The hardest crash in a NASCAR race since the installation of black boxes in the cars in 2001 was that of 128 g-force by Jerry Nadeau at Richmond International Speedway in 2003.

Lee Petty won the first Daytona 500 in 1959. Junior Johnson won the second.

Michael Waltrip holds the record for most starts without a win—463—before winning the Daytona 500 in 2001, the race in which Dale Earnhardt was killed.

No NASCAR drivers have been killed since the addition of neck and head restraints after the death of Earnhardt in 2001.

NASCAR drivers experience 3 g's of force on turns, about what astronauts on space shuttles feel on takeoff and reentry.

The first two Daytona 500 races were not five hundred miles.

Darlington Raceway in South Carolina was NASCAR's first superspeedway.

A superspeedway must be a minimum of two miles in length.

Talladega Superspeedway in Alabama is the longest superspeedway at 2.66 miles and has had the fastest recorded NASCAR speed of 228 miles per hour.

Temperatures can reach 170°F near the floorboards inside a NASCAR car.

NASCAR drivers can lose five to ten pounds of sweat during a race.

Janet Guthrie was the first woman to compete in the Daytona 500 and the Indianapolis 500.

Fred Marriott set the land speed record in 1906, going 127 miles per hour in a Stanley Steamer at Daytona Beach, Florida.

Englishman Andy Green became the first person to break the speed of sound on land, in 1997, reaching a speed of 763 mph at Black Rock Desert, Nevada.

EAR THEY GO

One of the events held at the World Eskimo-Indian Olympics is the ear pull, where heavy weights are hung from the earlobes with twine and the winning contestant must move forward the greatest distance.

GAME STOP

ANTE UP

Poker was invented by sailors in New Orleans in the 1820s. Originally, the game was played with three cards dealt from a deck of thirty-two.

Stud poker appeared around the time of the end of the Civil War.

The odds against a royal flush in five-card poker hands are 649,739 to 1.

The odds against a straight flush are 72,192 to 1.

The odds against four of a kind are 4,164 to 1.

The odds against a full house are 693 to 1.

The odds against a flush are 508 to 1.

The odds against a straight are 254 to 1.

GAMES PEOPLE PLAY

The board game Stratego was based on an old Chinese game called Jungle that used animal pieces instead of soldiers. It was designed by Mademoiselle Hernance Edan in 1909 as L'attaque.

Candy Land was the most popular board game of the 1940s. It was invented by Eleanor Abbott in 1945 while she was recovering from polio in San Diego.

Risk was created by a French movie director named Albert Lamorisse in 1957. He called the original game *La Conquête du Monde,* meaning "The Conquest of the World."

Life (or The Game of Life) was invented by Milton Bradley in 1860 as "The Checkered Game of Life." It sold forty-five thousand copies in its first year.

Parcheesi is the Americanized version of the ancient Indian game Pachisi, first played around 500 BC. The game was played by royalty, using real people in colorful costumes as the pieces on a giant outdoor board.

The board game Pay Day debuted in 1975 and outsold Monopoly in its first year.

Rummikub was invented by Ephraim Hertzano, a Romanian Jew, during the 1940s, when the government outlawed card playing. He immigrated to Israel after World War II and began selling the games. Rummikub was the top-selling game in the United States in 1977.

The word "Jenga" is from the Swahili word *kujenga*, meaning "to build."

Twister did not become a hit until Johnny Carson played the game with Eva Gabor on *The Tonight Show* in 1966.

Some critics accused Twister of being "sex in a box."

The dice game Yahtzee is said to have been invented in 1959 by a Canadian couple aboard their yacht.

TRIPLE WORD SCORE

Scrabble was invented by architect Alfred Mosher Butts, in 1938. The game, which he called "Criss-Cross Words," was based on an earlier word game he had created called Lexiko.

Butts came up with the letter frequency for Scrabble by analyzing how often letters appeared in various sources, including the *New York Times*.

Butts had no luck selling his game idea to Parker Brothers or Milton Bradley and eventually sold its rights to James Brunot in 1948. Brunot changed the name to Scrabble, which is a real word meaning "to scratch frantically."

It wasn't until Jack Strauss, the president of Macy's, played the game on vacation and loved it that Brunot found an outlet for Scrabble.

IN THE LIBRARY . . .

The murder mystery game Clue was originally called Murder and was invented by Anthony Pratt, a solicitor's clerk in England during World War II, for civilians to play while waiting in underground bunkers during German air raids.

The game is known as Cluedo in Europe.

ART IMITATES LIFE

In 1999, one astute player of the art auction game Masterpiece in Indiana noted that a painting used to cover a hole in his wall resembled a painting by Martin Johnson Heade depicted in the game. He had the work appraised and sold it to an art museum for $1.25 million.

WEDGIES

Twenty million Trivial Pursuit games, where players answer questions and collect wedges, were sold in North America in 1984 alone.

In that same year, Fred L. Worth, author of *The Trivia Encyclopedia* and other trivia books, sued the distributors of Trivial Pursuit, claiming that 25 percent of the facts in the original Genus Edition of the game were taken from his book, which they were. The case went all the way to the U.S. Supreme Court. Worth lost because facts cannot be copyrighted.

YOU SUNK MY BATTLESHIP!

Battleship was originally a paper-and-pencil game invented in the early 1900s by Clifford Von Wickler. He never patented his creation and Milton Bradley released their paper-and-pencil version in 1931, with the now familiar board game coming out in 1967.

OH, BABIES!

Ty Warner, the guy who invented and marketed Beanie Babies, is now a billionaire who owns the Four Seasons Hotel in New York.

BASICALLY BARBIE

Barbie's official birth date is March 9, 1959, the date that the doll debuted at the American International Toy Fair in New York.

> Barbie's siblings over the years have been Skipper; twins Todd and Tutti; Stacie, who replaced Tutti as Todd's twin sister; Kelly; and Krissy. She also has a cousin, Francie.

Barbie's parents are George and Margaret.

> Ken's last name is Carson.

Barbie was featured in a series of novels published by Random House in the 1960s.

Barbie's eyes did not face straight ahead until 1971. Before this, they looked slightly down and to the side.

WRIGHT ON!

John Lloyd Wright, son of famed architect Frank Lloyd Wright, invented Lincoln Logs in 1918.

The Lincoln Log design was taken from his father Frank Lloyd Wright's use of interlocking beams in the basement of the Imperial Hotel in Tokyo, to make it earthquake-proof.

The name Lincoln has nothing to do with Abraham Lincoln, who was born in a log cabin. Instead it was taken from the given middle name of Frank Lloyd Wright, which was Lincoln. He changed it to Lloyd, his mother's maiden name, after his father deserted the family.

ACKNOWLEDGMENTS

I'd like to thank my editor, Jeanette Shaw, for all her hard work and insights on making this series be the best it can be. Also, I want to acknowledge the very thorough efforts of this book's copyeditor, Rick Willett, and Sarah Romeo for the really fun cover design. And to my "incredible" literary agent, Janet Rosen—all your efforts on my behalf are greatly appreciated.

ABOUT THE AUTHOR

Don Voorhees has been fascinated by "useless" bits of information from a very young age. Happily, he found a use for all his accumulated trivial knowledge in his writings. This is Don's tenth book and it gives him great pleasure to share his love of "worthless" facts with his readers.

Don was born and raised in Morris County, New Jersey, and studied biology at Drew University and Rutgers. He now resides in eastern Pennsylvania with his wife, Lisa, and their two children, Eric and Dana.